Infusion

Infusion

Receive.

Grow.

Give It Away...

Jack Redmond

BRIDGE LOGOS FOUNDATION

Alachua, Florida 32615

Bridge-Logos
Alachua, FL 32615 USA

Infusion
by Jack Redmond

Edited by Mary Ruth Murray

Copyright ©2010 by Bridge-Logos

Printed in the United States of America.

Library of Congress Catalog Card Number: 2010925722
International Standard Book Number 978-0-88270-441-8

G616.316.N.m1004.35230

Contents

Foreword

Jack Redmond's concentration is on the heart of God—and the redemptive passion of God has always been the reaching and rescuing of lost people. Jack's heart rings loud and clear in this work. *Infusion* offers a prophetic sense of urgency. It calls you back to God … back to the singular focus of soul-winning … and back to a lifestyle that captures holy moments when God nudges you to receive, grow, and give away His message of love to a lost and dying world.

Although much has been done for Christ throughout the world—including the building of hospitals and orphanages, actions of social justice, and the hosting of great soul-winning crusades—the mandate to help lost people to connect with God still requires fulfillment.

I have served as Jack's pastor since the first day of his spiritual conversion in the summer of 1997. This privilege has afforded me the opportunity to see God shape his spiritual perspective, passion, and life-mission. I am thankful Jack has not taken his focus off of the Great Commission. As you read *Infusion*, you will rediscover why and how to connect with people for whom Jesus willingly died at Calvary.

David D. Ireland, Ph.D.
Senior Pastor, Christ Church
Author of *Journey to the Mountain of God*

Get in the Game

Chapter 1

Get in the Game!

Infusion is the process by which a substance is injected into something in order to increase its effectiveness or to bring change. When we look at our society, it is evident that we are in desperate need of an injection of Jesus Christ into our culture. It is painfully clear that many individuals are living outside of God's love and purposes. There are countless people who don't know about the love of God and His plans. There are others who just don't care. God, however, is different.

God cares about people. He not only cares for all people, but He deeply loves them. God not only loves people, but the Bible tells us that God is love (see 1 John 4:8). He not only has the emotion of love, He actually is love. If you were able to put God under a microscope, you would see that He is made of love. If you were able to dissect God the way you dissect a frog in science class, you would literally be pulling pieces of love out. If you could slice God like you slice a cake, you would have a slice of love on your plate.

We live in a world that is desperately searching for love. We search for love because there is an empty spot inside each of us that can only be filled with love. It cannot be filled with just any type of love; the only thing that can fill this empty spot completely is the perfect, unending, unconditional love of God.

God Extends His Love to All Mankind

The will of God is to reach every single person on the planet with this love. Sounds like a big task, but He is a big God. God is amazing in the way He does things. Many times God does things in ways we could never imagine. He personally reaches out to everyone; He also chooses to work through average people like you and me instead of just doing it himself. I don't always understand why He does it this way, but He does.

One of the reasons God works through everyday people like you and me is because much is achieved in the process. We learn about Him, grow closer to Him, and we become transformed to be more like Him. His goal at the end of the day is for us to have a relationship with Him, and that can only happen when we work with Him and He works in us, through us, and with us.

God teaches us that we are His ambassadors and that He speaks through us: *"We are therefore Christ's ambassadors, as though God were making his appeal through us"* (2 Corinthians 5:20). It amazes me that the God of the universe could do anything He wants, but He chooses to work through average people like you and me to achieve the miraculous. This also allows us to embark on a great adventure as we do mighty things on His behalf.

God Is Not That Complicated

People often make God complicated. In some ways there are things about God that we will spend eternity learning, but in many cases, God is very simple. I continually strive to explain God in a way that each individual can understand. People have made Christianity very complicated by the way things are taught, how people are trained, and the manner in which ministry often takes place. I believe much of this is man-made and, at times, unnecessary. Even the word *Christian* has become complicated. In fact, there are times when I don't like the word because it has so many different meanings, and sometimes no meaning at all.

Being a Christ-follower

A simpler way to look at faith is whether or not someone is a Christ-follower. There are many "Christians" who are not necessarily Christ-followers. Someone who follows Christ will do the things Christ did and over time will begin to act and be like Him. So the question becomes, "How do we do that?" I believe that it can be summed up with a little statement:

Receive. Grow. Give it away...

True Christianity is a process of ongoing growth and transformation. Transformation begins when we receive from God. As we receive love, forgiveness, and purpose, we grow in our understanding and live these things out in a greater way. These changes then cause such a blessing in our lives that the natural thing to do is to share or give them away to others. Along the way, we learn who God is and what He does. One of the easiest ways to describe God is that He is a giver.

> *For God so loved the world that he gave his one and only Son, that whoever believes in him shall not perish but have eternal life.* (John 3:16)

> *Yet to all who received him, to those who believed in his name, he gave the right to become children of God—children born not of natural descent, nor of human decision or a husband's will, but born of God.* (John 1:12-13)

> *For God's gifts and his call are irrevocable.* (Romans 11:29)

God gave us His Son, eternal life, gifts, and much more. If God is a giver, we must be receivers. Whenever God gives us something, it is for a purpose. He provides to meet our needs, to overcome personal struggles or pain, but also to empower us to change the world around us. This often involves a process. We must grow, and this takes time. God first gives us things like forgiveness, salvation, peace, or even healing. We receive these gifts, then they become more real and powerful as they bring change to our lives. As we grow and learn, our normal response is to share what we have learned and experienced with others.

4

God Is Looking for Receivers

I have heard preachers talk about the Church and how fat it is because all it does is receive and it never gives anything away. Often, I think this is correct, but I also believe that too many people are not really receiving everything God has for them. I think people sit in church like it is a restaurant and just get the appetizer, but they're missing the meat, potatoes, and vegetables that God has for them. If we are truly receiving everything that God has for us, we will be like the prophet who said the Word of God was like fire shut up in his bones.

But if I say, "I will not mention him or speak any more in his name," his word is in my heart like a fire, a fire shut up in my bones. I am weary of holding it in; indeed, I cannot. (Jeremiah 20:9)

The Apostle Paul also wrote, *"Woe to me if I do not preach the gospel,"* (1 Corinthians 9:16). I believe we would turn the world upside down if we each had this attitude, which resulted from being so filled with God and His Word that we just had to tell people about Jesus.

My prayer is that we would be like Paul and Jeremiah—that we would be so filled with the Spirit of God and His Word that we would overflow and could not contain it. This means that we need to grow as receivers. Too many of us are not giving away because we have nothing left to give. The little that we have received is used up in our daily struggles and there is nothing left to share with others. Some of us need to stop walking around and feeling bad because we are not doing enough, and start growing as receivers so that we have more than enough to give away.

From Receiving to Growing

We are God's vessels of hope and healing to a hurting world. God not only gives things to us to bless us, but so that we can be a blessing to others. Our greatest joy, healing, and fulfillment don't occur when we are receiving, but when we are growing and giving to others. There is a joy that only comes when we see God changing lives through our efforts when they are backed by His power.

Demonstration of Power

For the kingdom of God is not a matter of talk but of power. (1 Corinthians 4:20)

God isn't some religious symbol or man-made idea. He is the Creator of Heaven and Earth who rules the entire universe. He wants to demonstrate His power in each of our lives every day.

I met a young man who insisted that Jesus was successful in spreading His message because He was popular. There were times when Jesus was very popular but other times when He was not. As the discussion progressed, I shared with the young man that I didn't think that Jesus was successful because He was popular. I said that He was popular because He was powerful. When people are going through life's struggles and trials, they need power to overcome. Jesus was radically different from passive religion with its do's and don'ts, which had no power for real transformation. God has His do's and don'ts because He knows certain things are good for us and others aren't. Sometimes these things don't make sense, but when Jesus comes into our lives, He begins to change the way we think and He gives us the power to overcome and to live the right way. Jesus had power, His followers had power, and the same power is available for us today.

In a world that is looking for answers and solutions, it's our job to connect people with Jesus. For this to happen, we have to first receive Jesus for ourselves. After that, He leads us and trains us. This is a growth process. In a sense, we become experts through our experience so that we can help others.

Continuous Growth Over Time

Scripture teaches us about growth. In the Old Testament, Samuel was a prophet who started serving God as a small boy and became the most powerful prophet in the nation. In fact, he is the one who anointed Israel's first king, Saul, and later anointed David to be king over all Israel. But it all began with a small boy who made a decision to serve God as he grew up.

> *And the boy Samuel continued to grow in stature and in favor with the LORD and with men.* (1 Samuel 2:26)

Jesus followed a similar path in His lifetime.

And Jesus grew in wisdom and stature, and in favor with God and men. (Luke 2:52)

Jesus is our role model, and we should be growing in wisdom, in stature (if we have not reached full growth), and in the favor of God and man. Over time, we should be getting wiser. God's power and provision should become more evident, and we should be seeing favor and goodwill from people. All these demand growth. The difference between physical and spiritual growth is that spiritual growth must be on purpose. As a child, we ate food, went to sleep, and grew. We weren't trying to grow every day; it just happened. Spiritual growth is different because it is intentional. There is no way to accidentally grow spiritually. We grow on purpose and, in fact, the more we focus on growth, the more we will grow.

We Are Growing So That We Can Be More Like Christ

The truth is that we begin to act and are shaped by those with whom we spend our time. I once watched a cartoon about people and their dogs, and the amusing thing was that each dog and its owner looked alike. It's funny because I have also seen this in real life. The whole point of following Christ and spending time with Him through prayer and studying God's Word is for us to be transformed.

Spiritually, we have been created in the image of God. "Image" means exact likeness. We were created to be like God, but through our sin and bad choices, we were transformed into something much different. But once we start walking with Jesus, the change is on. Day by day, week by week, year by year we are supposed to change. The more we want to change, the quicker the process will be.

Most people do not like change. It is amazing how much people resist change, and this keeps us from living the life that God created us to live. It's not that God doesn't want to do amazing things in our lives; we just think that they will happen no matter what. This is simply not true. The more dedicated we are and the more we pursue Christ, the more we will be like Him. Paul wrote:

Instead, speaking the truth in love, we will in all things grow up into him who is the Head, that is, Christ. (Ephesians 4:15)

Paul was letting the Church of Ephesus know that it was time to grow up. It was time to be honest with themselves and with each other. He instructed them to share the truth in a way that was packaged in love so it would cause a gentle confrontation that would result in maturity.

Salvation Is Only the Start Line

Too many people think that after they have received Jesus as their Lord and Savior, the race has been completed. But this is only the start line. Can you imagine if you were at a track meet and the starter's gun sounded and the fastest person exploded off the start line, took three steps, stopped, and proudly declared, "I won!"? All the while, everyone else is running down the track. That may sound funny, but our churches are filled with people who stopped growing years ago. This should not be.

For therein is the righteousness of God revealed from faith to faith: as it is written, The just shall live by faith. (Romans 1:17, KJV)

The reality is that the closer we walk with God and the longer we continue to, God reveals himself to us more and more. The more we know and understand God, the greater our faith becomes and the more we will experience the power of God in our lives. It's kind of like climbing a mountain. The higher we go, the more exhilarating it becomes. The more we know God, the more exciting it gets, but we have to keep climbing.

Now the Lord is that Spirit: and where the Spirit of the Lord is, there is liberty. But we all, with open face beholding as in a glass the glory of the Lord, are changed into the same image from glory to glory, even as by the Spirit of the Lord. (2 Corinthians 3:17-18, KJV)

People claim they want freedom, but freedom only comes through growth. As we continue to grow in the image of God, we continually leave behind the things of the flesh that keep us in bondage to this world. But, once again, it is like climbing. Being transformed to be like Christ is like walking up a long flight of steps. Each step takes us a little higher. It may seem tedious and harder as time goes by, but if we keep climbing, we will reach our destination.

> *Like newborn babies, crave pure spiritual milk, so that by it you may grow up in your salvation, now that you have tasted that the Lord is good.* (1 Peter 2:2-3)

Remember that salvation is only the beginning of our relationship with Jesus. This Scripture tells us that we need to grow up in our salvation. In one way, salvation is instant in the sense that when we choose to follow and obey Jesus and ask for forgiveness of our sin, forgiveness is instantly granted and we begin a new life with Jesus as the center. Spiritual milk is the basic principles and teachings of God's Word, the Bible. Just like a baby grows stronger from constantly drinking the mother's milk, we can grow strong by constantly feeding our spiritual growth through taking in God's Word. God wants to transform us from spiritual babies to spiritual powerhouses. If we want to grow up, we must make sure that we are positioning ourselves to receive God's wisdom, power, and direction in life.

> *But grow in the grace and knowledge of our Lord and Savior Jesus Christ. To him be glory both now and forever! Amen.* (2 Peter 3:18)

Part of growing up spiritually is growing in the grace and knowledge of Jesus Christ. The word *grace* covers a lot of territory. One of the ways to understand God's grace is that He gives us the ability to do things we cannot do on our own and receive things above and beyond what we actually deserve.

The more knowledge we gain about Jesus, the greater our faith and trust in Him will become. This results in greater obedience, which positions us to walk in increased power and authority as we submit to His lordship in every area of our lives. When we live in His power and authority, we bring Him glory. As Jesus is glorified through our lives, others will be drawn to Him, resulting in their salvation and this same process begins in their lives. God's plan is that this process continues in our lives as we share the hope, power, purpose, and love of Jesus Christ with the people we touch each day.

And the child grew and became strong in spirit; and he lived in the desert until he appeared publicly to Israel. (Luke 1:80)

This Scripture is talking about John the Baptist and it describes how John went through a time of spiritual growth. Later on, he lived out God's purpose in a powerful way because he had grown up spiritually. John's mission was to go before Jesus and introduce what Jesus was going to do during His earthly life. God is looking for individuals who are willing to engage in a season of growth. Many people never live out the great adventures that God has already prepared for them because they never embrace the growth process.

We are all impressed with John the Baptist's life, but very few of us think about the process he went through to have that life. Everyone wants to be a spiritual champion, but there is a road that must be traveled to get there. In the 2008 Olympics, American swimmer Michael Phelps won a record eight gold medals. Everyone wants to cheer when the race is on, but the reality is that Michael won those gold medals one day at a time by training six hours a day. You can be a spiritual champion, but you have to be willing to pay a price and go through the process. God wants to prepare you. If you are willing to pay the price, you can get ready for a powerful life-changing ministry to take place in your life.

Chapter 2

The Power of Personal Ministry

God created us for greatness. He wants to do mighty things both in us and through us. We have been created with a plan and purpose. He is the Creator of this plan and purpose and He is also our personal guide along the path to greatness. Achieving greatness is a process that takes time. For our purposes, greatness must also be defined as "great in His kingdom." This may or may not mean the world will esteem or value what we do, but that does not matter. We are here to do God's will, not to please man. God is a God of greatness and when we do His will, great things will be done in and through our lives.

The main purpose for Jesus coming to Earth was to connect us with our Creator. Outside of this connection we will live our lives in our own strength and creativity. While God gives us tremendous abilities, our greatest moment in our own strength is only the beginning of what He wants to do in our lives.

Jesus not only showed us how to live, but He also showed us the process of how to change the world. First, it involves obedience to God. When we walk in obedience, we walk in God's power. Obedience is simply agreeing with God and partnering with Him to do what He desires. When we are in line with God's will, we gain access to His power. The same power that brought everything into creation and brought life into the world, then backs up our words and actions. God has already prepared work for us to do.

For we are God's workmanship, created in Christ Jesus to do good works, which God prepared in advance for us to do. (Ephesians 2:10)

Ministry Is Not a Position But a Lifestyle

Every person has been created for ministry. Ministry is our service to our fellow man that helps them connect with God and accomplish what God created them to do. This has been distorted over time. There was a fundamental shift from followers of Christ being actively involved in ministering to everyone they came in contact with, to a system in which one person ministers to a large group of people who receive what is said, apply it to themselves, and have it go no further.

When Jesus came and the early Church was established, there was not a hierarchal organizational structure between what we would view today as common believers and those who serve in full-time ministry. There were leaders established by God, but all were ministers. Everyone

16

ministered, not by profession, but by the common faith they endeavored to share with the world.

> *But you are a chosen people, a royal priesthood, a holy nation, a people belonging to God, that you may declare the praises of him who called you out of darkness into his wonderful light.* (1 Peter 2:9)

Christians are meant to be a nation of believers. God looks at all who follow Christ as priests with a duty to serve. The Church is at its greatest when individuals embrace the call of God on their lives and allow themselves to be used by God to do mighty deeds in their daily lives. In the early Church, people were drastically changed by their personal relationship with Jesus. Once they were changed, they simply shared with others what God had done in their lives.

> *Every day they continued to meet together in the temple courts. They broke bread in their homes and ate together with glad and sincere hearts, praising God and enjoying the favor of all the people. And the Lord added to their number daily those who were being saved.* (Acts 2:46-47)

This is the picture of what God wants to do today. He wants us to meet in churches, but in addition there should be ministry taking place every day. We should be touching people's lives in our schools, on the job, in all types of public settings, and in the privacy of our homes. When this happens, God adds souls to His kingdom daily. God wants to continually reach more people, and not just on Sunday mornings. God's will is that every single person on the planet comes into a personal relationship with Jesus Christ—and it's going to take all of us to reach everyone.

> *The Lord is not slow in keeping his promise, as some understand slowness. He is patient with you, not wanting anyone to perish, but everyone to come to repentance.* (2 Peter 3:9)

Repentance simply means changing the direction of your life and turning it toward God. It means people decide to follow God's way instead of their own way, or the way that the world tells them to go. It simply means making the decision to walk in God's plan and purpose. Each of us has a group of people that we can influence. God will use these relationships to help people connect with Him. God loves when we come together on Sunday morning to worship Him as the pastor shares a message from His Word. He loves to see people come together to grow. The problem is that Sunday morning is not enough. There are people who will never come to a church to hear the message of God's love, purpose, and hope. Another reality is that God wants to reach people every day from all walks of life. This is where regular people like you and me can do great things for God.

> *Day after day, in the temple courts and from house to house, they never stopped teaching and proclaiming the good news that Jesus is the Christ.* (Acts 5:42)

The Culture Shift in Christianity

This pattern changed significantly in the fourth century when Constantine, the Roman emperor, made Christianity the state religion of the empire. Before this, Christians were not held in high esteem by most people. They were a group of people who went around talking and teaching about a Man crucified on a Cross. Many were outcasts and even persecuted or killed for their faith. But their personal experience with Jesus was so powerful that they didn't mind the rejection, persecution, and, in some cases, death. Constantine changed things by building beautiful cathedrals. This had a widespread effect. First, it brought a level of respectability to Christianity that it had never experienced. The result was a shift from people who had become Christians because of a powerful spiritual experience that must be shared with others, to people getting involved for different reasons, such as social or political gain, or simply because it became the "right" thing to do. This took away the power and passion in many people. Secondly, and more devastating, was that a hierarchal structure was established in a way that made ordinary believers the type of second-class citizens who weren't allowed or required to minister in their daily lives.

The Shift From Powerful Ministers to Spectators

Instead of five hundred powerful people sharing their faith with everyone they knew, those same five hundred people began to go to a beautiful cathedral where they were taught by one man. Five hundred ministers now became five hundred spectators. This became the model of Christianity where followers of Christ became spectators with no power and for many, no personal experience to share. This eventually led to Roman Catholicism, which, combined with a period of illiteracy among the people, resulted in the practice that only priests were allowed to read and teach the Bible. The royal priesthood of every believer was reduced to the priesthood of the few.

The Reformation Brings Some Change

During the Reformation in the 1500s, the Bible was returned to the people along with the teaching of personal conversion, but the cathedral structure, for the most part, remained intact. But praise God that He is a God of restoration and He is in the process of bringing the ministry of the ordinary believer back. We see this throughout the world as followers of Jesus Christ are embracing the biblical model of ministry in which every believer is responsible for the Great Commission.

Then Jesus came to them and said, "All authority in heaven and on earth has been given to me. Therefore go and make disciples of all nations, baptizing them in the name of the Father and of the Son and of the Holy Spirit, and teaching them to obey everything I have commanded you. And surely I am with you always, to the very end of the age." (Matthew 28:18-20)

20

To reach the whole world, it is going to take all of us. For far too long, we have tried to complete the Great Commission through a few great men and women. We need these great men and women, and thank God for them, but they can't do it alone. Remember, it is God's will that every single human being on the planet has a personal relationship with Jesus, so that every person spends eternity in Heaven with God. For two thousand years, God's leaders have worked feverishly to spread the gospel to the ends of the Earth. If every follower of Jesus took the Great Commission personally, it could be fulfilled in a very short time. There are varying statistics on the number of Christians worldwide. A conservative number is that there are one billion born-again believers in the world out of a total population of about six billion people.

Worldwide Evangelism in Three Years

Imagine if those one billion believers dedicated one year to winning one person to Christ and then helping them grow. In one year, one billion would grow to two billion. If those two billion believers dedicated the next year to winning one person to Christ, the number would grow to four billion by the second year. If this continued for a third year, with every Christian committed to reaching one person for Christ, in the third year literally everyone on the face of the Earth could be won for Christ! This is the power of personal ministry. We must get away from the practice of one pastor, who is overworked and burnt-out, trying to serve both his church and the community. The reason why the average church in America has about seventy-five members is because they are following the model of one leader serving the whole church, instead of those seventy-five people embracing personal ministry and reaching their communities.

I thank God for the powerful leaders in our churches, but we have been asking them to do too much. Far too often, instead of focusing on their strengths, they spend the majority of their time and energy doing other things. The result is obvious. Many pastors are overwhelmed by all the responsibility, and discouraged because they are not spending their time and energy using their gifts. This should not be. Instead of one person carrying the workload, we should each lend a hand, use our gifts, and work together to build God's family through the local church.

So how does this take place? First we must shift our thinking back to a New Testament model of common followers of Christ doing the work of Christ.

> *"I tell you the truth, anyone who has faith in me will do what I have been doing. He will do even greater things than these, because I am going to the Father."* (John 14:12)

This Scripture is a powerful reminder to us that God created us to do great things. In fact it teaches us that we will do the same things that Jesus did. It is also very clear that this is not for the special few. Jesus said, *"anyone who has faith in me." Anyone* covers a lot of territory. This encourages me greatly. It tells me I don't have to be somebody special; I just have to have faith. I may not be somebody in the world, but I sure am *anyone*. The world often tells us that we must look a certain way, have certain credentials, backgrounds, connections, etc., but that is not God's way. He says *anyone* and He means it. This is far different from our traditional church structure.

The modern missionary structure demonstrates this transition. In the past, to be a missionary, a person had to first go to a four-year Bible college and then spend two to three years in additional missionary training before going to the mission field. This meant a seven-year training period before people actually went into ministry. While I believe that we should all get as much training as possible through the local church, Bible college, or seminary, these are not for every person. During those seven years of training, many people were discouraged, got sidetracked by life, and never made it into the mission field.

Missionary training has changed dramatically, especially with short-term missions. Short-term mission trips often begin with a couple of days of training and then a seven-to-ten day mission trip. The focus is on teaching a few specifics and then allowing people to get into the action. These people often serve tremendously well and they themselves are radically changed. They then go back home and are active in ministry with their friends and family. Some do greater missions work or full-time ministry in the years to come. God works powerfully in those who are willing to be used.

While we shouldn't be too quick to put people in leadership positions of authority, we do need to release people to influence those in their social circles with the Gospel of Christ. Some of the greatest witnesses for God are those who are newly saved. They might not know much, but they know God is real and He changes lives. It is the job of the more mature to disciple and oversee their actions and to lend a helping hand when needed. We often wait for people to become mature believers. Too many times this results in their attending the church for a while and becoming very comfortable being spectators.

The Importance of Church Leaders

So since we are getting everyday followers of Christ to do ministry, should we get rid of the pastors and other leaders in the Church? Absolutely not! As we see more people ministering, our leaders don't become obsolete, they become more important.

It was he who gave some to be apostles, some to be prophets, some to be evangelists, and some to be pastors and teachers, to prepare God's people for works of service, so that the body of Christ may be built up. (Ephesians 4:11-12)

These leaders listed have what are called the fivefold ministry gifts. These are specific callings that certain people receive. When you see great leaders in the Body of Christ, they are usually operating in one of these gifts and are able to affect large numbers of people. However, their primary role is to train others to do on a personal level what they do on a public level. The job of a great Bible teacher is to equip people to share the truth of God's Word from their hearts. The job of an apostle is to supervise a region in establishing and overseeing churches to function on the local level in training believers to minister from house to house as the early Church did.

24

Sunday Morning—the Church As a Training Center

Sunday church is not just a time to come together and receive a lesson or an encouraging message so that we can feel good for the rest of the week. While those things should happen, something more important should be taking place. When we go to church we go to be trained and equipped to change the world. We should go to church with an expectation that we will learn or gain something that will help us minister to people.

The problem is, for many of us, Sunday morning is the time to be a spectator and to be fed. However, the true purpose of being spiritually fed is to be strengthened to do the work of ministry. Sunday morning should be the time we go the place where we are trained to achieve something great. Many of us have played sports and have been coached to be victorious on the field. Or we have had training sessions at work to focus on achieving a goal at our jobs. By the same token, going to church is the opportunity to learn God's ways (our game plan) and to be trained on how to be victorious (overcoming the devil's plans and schemes), not only in our lives, but to be able to share what we have learned with the world.

The most powerful force on the planet is a group of believers who have decided to do the work of God and are backed by His power. It begins with strong leaders who will train people to do the work of ministry. It continues when individuals answer the call of God and make the choice to be built up and sent out to share Christ with a searching world. While the leaders in the church are the generals, it is the congregants in the church who are the foot soldiers and platoon leaders. They are the ones who really do the work that leads to victory outside the walls of the church. God is looking for people to change the world. He will bring you through the process. You just need to say yes to whatever God has for you. I don't know what God has already planned for you to do, but I guarantee it will be the greatest adventure you could ever have. We've been built up. We've been called. Let's get in the game!

Chapter 3

From Spectator to Game-winner

Christianity is in need of a serious tune-up. Too many Christ-followers have been spectators for far too long. I thank God for the many men, women, teens, and children who are serving God in a powerful way. I thank God for the many ministers and churches who are sharing the gospel and meeting needs in the families and churches in their communities. But there is so much more God wants to do. If we want to see individuals, families, and our communities won to the Lord, we have to get in the game. Too many people are sitting around and asking why God isn't doing something, when He is ready and waiting for people like you and me to tell Him, "Use me."

The longer I serve Christ, the more I realize I am only beginning to see the magnificent things that God wants to do. God lets us know what our lives should look like for those who follow Christ:

Now to him who is able to do immeasurably more than all we ask or imagine, according to his

> *power that is at work within us, to him be glory
> in the church and in Christ Jesus throughout all
> generations, for ever and ever! Amen.* (Ephesians
> 3:20-21)

God is able and wants to do *"immeasurably more than
all we ask or imagine."* Does that describe your life? Many
times during leadership trainings, I have asked rooms full
of church leaders the question: "Does this Scripture describe the ministry that you oversee?" It's pretty interesting to watch people squirm nervously in their seats or look
down at the floor in response. If leaders of churches and
ministries aren't experiencing the power of God in its fullness, is it any wonder that the people in the congregation
aren't experiencing it either?

It is clear that God wants to do great things in our lives,
but many believers never experience it for themselves or
in their churches. This needs to change. I don't say these
things to shame people, but to begin to cause a shift in
the way they think. If we change the way we think, it will
change our expectations—which is another word for faith.
What is your expectation for God every day in your life?
Does it need a tune-up?

Believing for More

Many people interpret the Bible based on their
personal experience. When we do that, we often lower our
faith expectations because of our past personal experience.
"Jesus Christ is the same yesterday and today and forever"
(Hebrews 13:8). Those who have faith in Jesus will do
the same things that He did and even greater things (see

John 14:12). Let's begin to pray that God will raise our experience to match the Bible, instead of watering down the Bible to match our past experiences. God is looking for people who will read His Word, believe His Word, speak His Word, and do His Word. When we do these things, we have the power of Almighty God behind us. It is not us who do the mighty deeds, but the power of God working within us.

Many faithful people who attend church every week and love the Lord are not seeing their friends and family come to Christ. People are struggling with fear and doubt and confusion because of the things that they lack in life. Many have lost the passion that they once had for Christ. It is not too late. When any of us makes a choice to seek and trust God in a greater way, He is waiting for us; and He always delivers.

Jesus Showed Us How to Change the World

It only took Jesus a few short years to demonstrate and teach us how to fulfill the Great Commission. Christianity in its simplest form is the most powerful force on Earth and is available to anyone who believes. The steps Jesus demonstrated were simple:

- He called the apostles to be with Him.

- He taught and demonstrated the power of God.

- He sent them out to teach and demonstrate the power of God to others.

- The apostles then taught others to have faith for miracles and power.

- This simple process is to be repeated until the entire world is reached.

This process reaches ordinary people from all walks of life. These people then reach out to those in their lives, or deliberately reach out to new people to continue the process. God empowers ordinary people like you and me to do extraordinary things that change the lives of the people we touch. Christianity, from its beginning, was about relationships and power. It was not respected by the established religious or political powers of the day, but it was unstoppable in changing and expanding lives as people were changed through its power.

There were times of great moves of God, like the Day of Pentecost, when three thousand people came to Christ. But those people didn't just rejoice that they found the true and living God. They then went from house to house to share Christ and His power. Shortly after the Day of Pentecost we see what happened: *"But many who heard the message believed, and the number of men **grew** to about five thousand"* (Acts 4:4, emphasis mine). There was no single move of God that we know of that added the two thousand new souls; just ordinary people sharing with others the Gospel of Jesus Christ and God's life-changing power. Over the next few centuries, Christianity continued to be a powerful move that was not respected by many, but undeniable to those it touched.

It's Time to Get in the Game

Many preachers are spending all of their time and energy trying to keep their church members happy and hoping a few more may join in the days to come. What is supposed to take place on Sunday morning is that the people listening in the pews are to be trained to do the work of ministry. The whole point of Sunday morning is not just to meet the needs of the people in attendance. The point is to train everyone so they can be sent out with the most powerful force in the universe within them and turn the world upside down.

Many people are sitting in churches who are very frustrated. They know in their souls that God has created them for something greater than they are currently experiencing. They are frustrated, discouraged, and some are even mad. Does this sound like anyone you know? The solution isn't getting a new pastor, a new church, or a new kind of experience. The solution is getting in the game, believing God to use you in the same way the twelve—and then the seventy-two—disciples were used when Jesus sent them out.

The seventy-two returned with joy and said, "Lord, even the demons submit to us in your name." (Luke 10:17)

It is time for you to be amazed.

Infusing the Purpose, Power, and Plans of Christ Into Our Culture

God wants to inject you—filled with His power— into a sin-sick and hurting world. Jesus is the answer, and you are the delivery system. Like medicine on a doctor's office shelf, it doesn't help anyone until it is injected, or infused, into people who are sick and brings the cure to their sickness. Let's end spectator Christianity and watch people's lives be revolutionized by Jesus Christ.

Amazing Christianity

Being a follower of Christ is the most dynamic, powerful, and exciting endeavor that a person can be involved in on this side of eternity. Nothing can transform lives, heal broken hearts, and help people live a life of purpose and power like Jesus Christ. But the reality is that this does not describe many Christians' lives. Many people view Christianity as going to church and living a moral life, but that is only a small part of it. Our churches should be the spiritual hospitals of society—loving, serving, and mending the broken. Not only that, but we should be making house calls and bringing much needed spiritual medicine to our neighborhoods and workplaces and the dark, dreary corners that our churches have been trying to hide from for too long.

It Will Take an Army

I often say that it is going to take everyone to reach everyone. Each of us has different personalities, backgrounds, and temperaments that can cause certain people to like us, and others to be uncomfortable with us. Every person is important because everyone is unique and gifted and able to reach different types of people. Each of us has qualities, because of who we are, that will open and close the doors of other people's lives. That is okay. God's army is a big team and the reality in a championship game is that it doesn't matter who makes the big plays as long as the team wins. Let's just focus on doing our part and winning as many people to Christ as we can. In eternity it won't matter who did what; it just matters who made it to Heaven. We are all God's spokesmen.

The Nameless, Faceless Move of God

Too many people are waiting for the next Billy Graham or T. D. Jakes to step forward and change the world. I thank God for men like these and believe there will always be powerful leaders who will be recognized for what God does through them. But I believe there is something more powerful than any one individual. And that is the cumulative efforts of simple Christians like you and me who may never be singled out or celebrated for what we do.

Don't wait for a title, position, or for someone to recognize and send you. All of these things have their place, and for good reason, but too many people limit themselves because they have not been recognized or given some title. Even when the seventy-two returned to Jesus and were amazed at the authority and power that God had given them, Jesus told them, *"However, do not rejoice that the spirits submit to you, but rejoice that your names are written in heaven"* (Luke 10:20). If you are a child of God, you are a co-heir with Christ and there is no greater title!

> *Now if we are children, then we are heirs—heirs of God and co-heirs with Christ, if indeed we share in his sufferings in order that we may also share in his glory.* (Romans 8:17)

Can you imagine if the one billion born-again believers alive today made a decision to get in the game, stop being spectators, and started sharing the gospel, praying for miracles, and walking in the authority of Christ? Ninety-nine percent of these ordinary people may never have a title, but their effect on the world would be more than what every person who has a title could do.

God created you to do mighty deeds. Make the decision today to receive everything that God wants to give you. Grow in what you have already received and then get ready to share it everywhere you go. This is God's game plan. Once you embrace it, your life will never be the same!

Chapter 4

From the Great Commission to the Great Fulfillment

Jesus gave us the Great Commission and almost two thousand years later there are billions of people who have not yet even heard His name. There are countless others who have heard the name of Jesus many times, but it doesn't mean anything to them. Even with technology, Christian television, radio, music, the Internet, and great men and women of God, this is still a reality. Though all these things are good and should be utilized, there is a simpler more effective method. This method is person-to-person.

Generational Ministry

Over the years in ministry, I have adopted 2 Timothy 2:2 as my lifetime Scripture:

And the things you have heard me say in the presence of many witnesses entrust to reliable men who will also be qualified to teach others.

The Apostle Paul is speaking to one of his key disciples, Timothy. He is letting the young pastor know that it is not good enough to just receive teaching yourself. It is a good start, but it shouldn't end there. True Christianity is demonstrated by ongoing generations of Christ-followers. It was not even enough in Paul's eyes to teach truths to someone else. Paul said to *"entrust* [these truths] *to reliable men who will also be qualified to teach others."* What this demonstrates is a multiplication, not of believers, but of ministers. It also builds a culture that is committed to an ever-expanding ministry designed to reach the ends of the Earth.

Growing the Family Tree

I remember drawing a poster of our family tree when I was a child. It is pretty amazing to see how in a few generations, a family tree can quickly grow and expand. Physically, this may take twenty-five to thirty years for each generation. Spiritually, this can be a lot faster and more far-reaching. I feel so strongly about this concept that I named my ministry Fourth Generation Ministries, which gets it's name from 2 Timothy 2:2. The Apostle Paul (first generation) taught Timothy (second generation), told him to entrust these truths to reliable men (third generation), who would be qualified to teach others (fourth generation). If you are a follower of Christ, you are literally one of the generations that followed the original apostles and Jesus himself.

Your Spiritual Family Tree

Statistics say that about 90 percent of Christians in America have never led anyone to Christ. This means that

90 percent of the people who have been taught about Jesus and received Him have kept Jesus to themselves and not effectively shared Him with others. So here is the question: What does your spiritual family tree look like? How many spiritual generations have you produced? Ninety percent of Christians are spiritually barren. In Bible days if you were physically barren, it was perceived as an appalling condition or circumstance. My prayer is that Christ-followers will have an even greater understanding of the devastating effect of spiritual barrenness. The reason sin is so rampant and tyranny exists around the world is because of the spiritual barrenness of millions of Christians over the past two thousand years. If every Christ-follower had committed to living a life of power and authority and then shared it with others, our world would be vastly different.

Becoming Spiritually Fertile

Remember that reproducing either physically or spiritually is not just for you. It is also for those you produce. You are a physical product of a physical act. If you have been born again, you are the product of a spiritual act, being born of the Spirit. You are also the product of someone sharing Christ with you. This may have been a pastor in a church or maybe a friend over a cup of coffee at a diner. Where you heard it and whom you heard it from doesn't matter; somebody explained God's plan to you and you accepted it. You may have a desire to see more lives changed than ever before through your personal ministry to others, or you may be hearing about this for the first time. Either way, God wants to make you more productive and more spiritually reproductive.

So the question is, "How do I do that?" The answer is simple. Put yourself in Timothy's place for a minute. Take what has been taught to you and teach it to others. Reproduction physically or spiritually is very simple: Take the life-giving substance in you and give it to someone else. Spiritually, this means sharing truth, love, and Jesus Christ with others. Take what is in you and give it to others.

Then if you want spiritual grandchildren, you must share with others in a way that enables them to share these same truths with others. This has been going on for two thousand years, from Jesus down to you and me today. When you do this, your influence will live far beyond your own lifetime and it will extend to others in ways you never dreamed possible.

Living Out Discipleship

Discipleship is really sharing our lives with others in a way that helps them live out the purpose for which God created them. It involves loving, caring, correcting, and training people. It also results in people pouring into others what they have received from you. As a minister, I have shifted my primary focus from teaching individuals to instructing leaders and spiritual mothers and fathers. When I am able to affect these people, I am able to affect everyone they influence. The more time I spend training leaders and mobilizing congregations, the greater my "Jesus footprint" will be. While your primary goal is to share Christ with any and everyone, make sure you focus your time and energy on those with the greatest gifts and passion to reach others. Too many ministers spend all their time helping those in crisis instead of pouring their efforts into the most spiritually fertile. They, in turn, can be trained to not only reproduce, but can also deal with the crises so many people face.

From Thought to Action

So at this point it all sounds good, but let's get to work. You are probably getting fired up to change the world. Or maybe you think it sounds good, but you don't know where to start. It's simple. If you want to help people and to give all you have to others, you must first have something to give.

Let's begin our journey of changing the world one person at a time. It will begin with you. It's great that you want to give yourself, your time, and your gifts to others. Let's first focus on having something to give. Let's get ready to receive.

Section 2

Receive

Chapter 5

Receiving Jesus

People can make God seem so complicated. In addition to that, we live in a complicated world. On top of that, we usually try to figure out everything on our own. I firmly believe that if we begin to understand the simple things about God, it will take away a great deal of the confusion about many other things. The clearer we see who God is, the clearer we will be able to see the world around us.

One of the first things we need to understand is God is a giver. The one Scripture that is quoted most often and known by so many people is John 3:16:

For God so loved the world that he gave his one and only Son, that whoever believes in him shall not perish but have eternal life.

This is the essence of giving.

In a world that can be complicated, one thing we can clearly see is that God is a giver. When God gave His only Son, He gave His best and what was most important to

Him in all of creation. When someone gives you the thing that matters most to them, you can be confident that that person is a giver. In a relationship if someone is giving something, for the process to be completed, someone must receive it. Receiving the gift completes the act of giving.

When we receive the gift of Jesus, we receive the gift of eternal life and a spiritual adoption takes place as God adopts us as His children.

> *For you did not receive a spirit of slavery to fall back into fear, but you have received a spirit of adoption. When we cry, "Abba! Father!"* (Romans 8:15, NRSV)

God actually chooses to adopt us and be our heavenly Father. But it begins with us receiving Jesus and believing in Him.

> *Yet to all who received him, to those who believed in his name, he gave the right to become children of God—children born not of natural descent, nor of human decision or a husband's will, but born of God.* (John 1:12-13)

Jesus is available to all people. God is not picky about who can receive Him. In fact, He wants all of us to receive Him. God receiving us is not a complicated process that only a few will ever know about or achieve. We don't have to bend over backward or do back flips; we just have to receive what God already wants to give us. Receiving Jesus happens when we believe He is who He says He is. By believing in His name, we are saying we recognize that

Jesus is the Messiah, the Son of God, God in the flesh, and we recognize and put our faith in those things as we receive the forgiveness of our sins and choose to follow Jesus as our Lord.

Something else also takes place. We are given rights as God's children.

It is that very Spirit bearing witness with our spirit that we are children of God, and if children, then heirs, heirs of God and joint heirs with Christ. (Romans 8:16-17, NRSV)

An heir is someone who receives an inheritance from another person. This usually occurs at the time of physical death when possessions and gifts are passed along to the next generation. This is different spiritually since God is never going to die. That means we are not waiting for a day of death; we can receive right now. God is ready not only to give eternal life to all who believe in His Son, but much more. But it all begins by receiving Jesus as our Lord and Savior.

Personally Receiving Jesus

God's children must be like Him. Due to our own actions and our own sin, we actually disqualify ourselves from being God's children. Scripture tells us that: *"All have sinned and fall short of the glory of God"* (Romans 3:23) and *"Your iniquities have separated you from your God; your sins have hidden his face from you* (Isaiah 59:2).

It has been our own sin that separates us from God. In the process of sinning, we give up our right to be God's children. Whether we know it or not, we are surrendering and forfeiting our right through the choices we make and the actions that follow. It is like a criminal who robs a store. He may know it is the wrong thing to do, or he might think it is okay because he needs the money. But once the crime is committed and he is caught and convicted, he will lose his rights. He will lose his right to freedom. He will lose his right to decide his own actions and will be told what to do and when to do it. He will lose access to his friends and family. In the same way, our sin causes us to lose access to God. After we lose this access, there is nothing we can do to regain it. We can only receive it through grace.

> For it is by grace you have been saved, through faith—and this not from yourselves, it is the gift of God—not by works, so that no one can boast. (Ephesians 2:8-9)

One of the simple ways we can explain grace is that grace is receiving that which we do not deserve. In this case, it is referring to forgiveness and eternal life with God in Heaven. We are saved from our own poor choices and actions through placing our faith in a loving Savior. This Scripture further explains that grace is a gift from God. Remember, God is a giver. We must also realize it does not depend on our own efforts. How good we are or have been is not something we can ever brag about. We must acknowledge that we had an eternal problem and Jesus came to get us out. But we have to receive it.

It's like going in the wrong direction on a highway, then making a U-turn and starting to go in the right direction. In our sin, we are literally spiritually dead. We are physically, emotionally, and psychologically alive; but we are spiritually dead. Then we receive Jesus, we receive forgiveness, and we receive spiritual life. We begin a new life. This is what it means to be born of God, or born again as Jesus told Nicodemus in John 3:3: *"In reply Jesus declared, 'I tell you the truth, no one can see the kingdom of God unless he is born again.'"*

We are born again through accepting Jesus as our Lord and Savior and receiving forgiveness for our sins. The journey that was leading us to death takes a U-turn, and we begin our journey of life. We make a spiritual U-turn and cross over to the highway going in the opposite direction.

> *"I tell you the truth, whoever hears my word and believes him who sent me has eternal life and will not be condemned; he has crossed over from death to life."* (John 5:24)

So our spiritual journey must begin with God as the giver and us as the receivers. We accept the payment for our sins and receive Jesus as our Lord and Savior. Forgiveness sets us free. Free from sin, free from guilt, and the control that those things have over our lives. There are too many people walking around dealing with guilt over the past. We have all made mistakes and have paid a price for them. Too many people have the paralyzing weight of the past on their backs and it keeps them from moving forward and achieving all that God has for them. We often live with the pain and reality of what we have done. We see the consequences of the choices we have made in our lives and in our relationships. Others will often remind us and hold these things against us. On top of that we have an enemy who is called Satan: *"... the accuser of our brothers, who accuses them before our God day and night"* (Revelation 12:10b).

Satan is a master manipulator and wants to use our past against us. If we are incapacitated by the past, we will never be able to achieve mighty things for God. Two of Satan's greatest weapons are guilt and shame. They are a trap and a type of prison, but Jesus came to set the captives free.

The Difference Between Conviction and Condemnation

Conviction is a process by which God shows us our sin so that we can recognize it, confess it, and be forgiven for it. God actually sends His Holy Spirit to do the work of conviction (see John 16:8). The opposite of conviction is denial. There are many people who deny that sin exists or that it doesn't matter, or they simply flat-out enjoy their sin and don't care what happens to them or the people around them.

Conviction is an act of love. God refuses to let us go down the wrong path that will destroy our lives now, and whose end is eternal separation from Him. Conviction is when God shines a light on what we are doing wrong so we can change.

Condemnation is a process that people actually choose and the devil promotes in every way he can. John 3:16 may be the most famous Scripture, but we need to keep reading so we can fully understand why God the Father sent Jesus.

"For God did not send his Son into the world to condemn the world, but to save the world through him. Whoever believes in him is not condemned, but whoever does not believe stands condemned already because he has not believed in the name of God's one and only Son. This is the verdict: Light has come into the world, but men loved darkness instead of light because their deeds were evil. Everyone who does evil hates the light, and will not come into the light for fear that his deeds will be exposed." (John 3:17-20)

So Jesus came to save the world, not to condemn it. Jesus is the light. This means He is the right way and that He shows us the right way. He not only shows us the right way, but He shines a light on the wrong things in our lives. We can choose to keep doing what is wrong and destructive, or see our actions for what they are and walk away from them. When our evil deeds are exposed, it can be a painful thing. We are given the choice of opening up the wounds of sin and allowing Jesus to clean them out or to pretend those wounds don't exist. Sometimes we pretend they don't exist because we like the temporary pleasure of our sin and want to keep doing it. Other times it is too painful to face the reality of what we have done. But if we truly want to be set free, we must face reality. Conviction shows us reality so we can make the adjustments we need to make. Godly conviction begins a process that leads to forgiveness and freedom.

Conviction is a type of sorrow for the sinful things we have done. It leads to confession, which leads to forgiveness, which leads to freedom. The opposite of conviction is condemnation. Condemnation doesn't say, "What I did was bad;" it says "I am bad." We are all created in the image of God and, in our pure essence, are good. It is sin that corrupts and damages us. Condemnation is not the process of helping us overcome and live a free and abundant life. It is a dead end; a bad place that keeps getting worse and worse. Condemnation is one of Satan's most powerful tools. It is like a cloud that follows you and surrounds you.

Living in a state of condemnation usually results in one of two consequences. Condemnation can either wear us down and hold us back, or, even worse, it can destroy our sense of right and wrong until we don't care what we do. It can also go back and forth between the two. As time goes on, people who live in a state of condemnation grow in their feelings of guilt, shame, and unworthiness. This can lead to either depression or denial of reality, which also leads to an uncaring attitude.

> ... *whose consciences have been seared as with a hot iron.* (1 Timothy 4:2b)

This Scripture refers to those who abandon true faith and live by false teaching or false understanding. Eventually they lose their ability to know or care about right and wrong. This is a dangerous place to be. As we look around the world, we can see this demonstrated by people who engage in all kinds of immorality and are not fazed by it.

Loving God, But Disliking Ourselves

There are also many others who truly want to serve God but are living in a state of condemnation. This is what Satan wants. He wants to cripple us in our emotions and thoughts so that we do not receive forgiveness and freedom. Then we cannot powerfully serve God or do our part to change the world. Forgiveness and the freedom to know and serve God are what drove Jesus to the Cross. Jesus came to save us from our sin, to break the power of condemnation, and to bring us into a life of ministry to do the works that He did. None of this can be accomplished without first receiving. That means first receiving Jesus as Lord and Savior—and that is just the beginning of more to come.

Receiving Jesus

If you have never asked Jesus to forgive your sins and then commit yourself to being a follower of His, you can do it right now. It's a simple choice. Either be forgiven or stay guilty in your sins. Either continue to run your own life, or follow the One who created you and let Him guide you into the true purpose for which you were created.

I made a choice to follow Jesus and ask for forgiveness in the summer of 1997. That decision radically changed me. For the first time in my life, I had peace on the inside. Jesus began to heal and direct me in the way I should go. I could endlessly try and explain it, but the only way for you to really understand is to begin the journey and live in relationship with Jesus yourself. We are saved by putting our trust in Jesus as Lord and Savior. *Lord* means He runs the show; He is in charge. *Savior* means He saves us from our sin because He went to the Cross to die for our sins so we can be forgiven. He leaves it up to us. If you have not begun this relationship with Jesus, you can begin it right now with a prayer:

Jesus,

I am tired of running my own life and I am tired of carrying around the weight of my sin. Today I choose to begin a relationship with you. I ask you to forgive my sin, come into my heart, and begin to direct my life. I commit to following you. Thank you for dying on the Cross for my sin and rising after three days to overcome death and the grave. Today I choose to overcome sin and the power it has on my life and follow you.

I pray this in Jesus' name. Amen.

If you prayed that prayer and meant it in your heart, God heard you, forgave you, and will lead you. You just received Jesus as your Lord and Savior. In the days ahead, you will grow in what that means and, finally, share the hope, love, and purpose of Jesus with others.

Chapter 6

Receiving the Holy Spirit

Remember that God is the greatest giver in existence. The greatest thing anyone can give is themselves. When God gives to us, it is not a matter of how much He will give, but how much we are willing and able to receive. In order to do the work of God, we need to have His power working through our lives. The way that God does this is to give us the Holy Spirit. For some people the idea of the Trinity is difficult to understand. The easiest way to explain it is there is one God, represented in three Persons: God the Father; God the Son (Jesus); and God the Holy Spirit. It should not surprise us that an infinite and all-powerful God may be beyond our limited understanding.

Once when I was speaking to a congregation during a Bible study I joked and said, "Let's be real. We sit at our kitchen tables and can't comprehend the riddles on the back of our kids' cereal boxes and then have a problem when we don't understand every single detail about the most amazing, infinite, and all-powerful God!" Jesus made it clear that He was sent by God the Father. He then sends us to continue His work, not in our own strength, but in the strength and power of the Third Person of the Trinity, the Holy Spirit:

> *Again Jesus said, "Peace be with you! As the Father has sent me, I am sending you." And with that he breathed on them and said, "Receive the Holy Spirit." (John 20:21-22)*

Again, the Bible records that Jesus is commanding His followers to continue His work, but through the power of the Holy Spirit. This power allows us to represent Jesus, locally, regionally, and even over the entire world.

> *"But you will receive power when the Holy Spirit comes on you; and you will be my witnesses in Jerusalem, and in all Judea and Samaria, and to the ends of the earth." (Acts 1:8)*

I am often amazed at the controversy and heated arguments that take place between Christians when it comes to the Holy Spirit. People argue about receiving the Holy Spirit, what that means, how it happens, and what the results are. To me, much of this confusion, and even arguing, isn't necessary. Let's focus on a few basic things.

Jesus said that we have to receive the Holy Spirit. To receive the Holy Spirit, we must want the Holy Spirit. In both of the Scriptures above, Jesus told His followers to receive the Holy Spirit, and, in another instance, that they would receive the Holy Spirit at a later time. As followers of Jesus and, in order to see God move powerfully in our lives, we must receive the Holy Spirit. This is first done when we decide to commit our lives to following Jesus.

Peter replied, "Repent and be baptized, every one of you, in the name of Jesus Christ for the forgiveness of your sins. And you will receive the gift of the Holy Spirit." (Acts 2:38)

To *repent* literally means to change direction. It means we are going in a direction that is somehow different from the direction God wants to lead us. We then voluntarily decide to stop going in that direction and turn to God and allow Him to lead us in the direction He would have us go. When we do this, God gives us the Holy Spirit to direct us on a daily basis and to keep us on the right path. I have heard people argue that when we are born again, we receive the Holy Spirit in 100 percent of the fullness that we ever will. I believe Scripture shows us something else. In the following Scripture, Peter came into contact with a group of people who had made decisions to follow Jesus. They had been baptized and, from what we know, were serving Jesus as best as they knew how. Peter recognized that these followers of Christ, for some reason, were not living in the full power of the Holy Spirit, and he prayed for them so they would receive the Holy Spirit.

When they arrived, they prayed for them that they might receive the Holy Spirit, because the Holy Spirit had not yet come upon any of them; they had simply been baptized into the name of the Lord Jesus. Then Peter and John placed their hands on them, and they received the Holy Spirit. (Acts 8:15-17)

It is possible for someone to be committed to following Christ but not to have received the Holy Spirit in a way that results in the type of power God wants to give us.

Acts 9:17 tells us to *"be filled with the Holy Spirit."* This literally means that we should keep on being filled and constantly be filled with the Holy Spirit. This is not a one-time experience. It means to get filled over and over again.

> *And if the Spirit of him who raised Jesus from the dead is living in you, he who raised Christ from the dead will also give life to your mortal bodies through his Spirit, who lives in you.* (Romans 8:11)

> *Don't you know that you yourselves are God's temple and that God's Spirit lives in you?* (1 Corinthians 3:16)

These two Scriptures teach us the amazing truth that when we choose to follow Christ, the Holy Spirit actually moves into our lives and literally lives within us. This is the source of ongoing power and ability to do the works of Christ. It is not our own strength, but the strength of God. This is why we should expect amazing things to happen through us. If the Holy Spirit has the power to raise Jesus from the dead after three days, He can surely help us in our struggles and tasks. God's Word also teaches us that our bodies are God's temple. This helps us to understand that it is not just up to us to get people into a church to connect with God, but that we have God himself within us so that we can take God to people right where they are.

Telling God That We Want More of the Holy Spirit

Even if you are wrestling with understanding the Holy Spirit—receiving Him, or being filled by Him—I think it is very clear we need Him and as much of Him as we can get. Instead of trying to argue out the details, let's just begin to ask God the Father to send us the Holy Spirit in a greater way. And let us continually surrender every area of our lives to God so He can work through us to do amazing things.

Remember, God is a giver and He keeps on giving. After we receive Jesus and the Holy Spirit, God wants to continue to bless us. We will see in the next chapter how we continue to receive when we commit to a life of prayer.

Chapter 7

Receiving Through Prayer

Almost everything we receive from God is in response to prayer. These prayers come from ourselves, from other people, through Jesus himself, and even the Holy Spirit. God can do anything He wants at any time, but the Bible teaches us that He responds to our prayers. He desires ongoing connection and communication with us, which occurs through prayer. Prayer also demonstrates our dependence on God instead of a foolish pride that thinks we can do anything or get anything on our own. Even when it seems like we get things through our own strength or talent, it is actually through utilizing the gifts God has given us.

In the Old Testament God often revealed who He was through a specific action or describing himself. One of those times God revealed himself as *Jehovah Jirah,* which means "the Lord, my provider." This lets us know He is the one we should go to when we have needs. In the gospels, Jesus teaches us that we should not be anxious like those who don't know Him:

"And why do you worry about clothes? See how the lilies of the field grow. They do not labor or spin. Yet I tell you that not even Solomon in all his splendor was dressed like one of these. If that is how God clothes the grass of the field, which is here today and tomorrow is thrown into the fire, will he not much more clothe you, O you of little faith? So do not worry, saying, 'What shall we eat?' or 'What shall we drink?' or 'What shall we wear?' For the pagans run after all these things, and your heavenly Father knows that you need them. But seek first his kingdom and his righteousness, and all these things will be given to you as well." (Matthew 6:28-33)

Receiving Through Personal Prayer

God's plan is that we come to Him in prayer. Many times we don't have what we need personally or we are not achieving what God has created us to do, all because we have not asked for them in prayer. A young woman in our church shared that when she asked for something in prayer she felt selfish because she was fairly well off financially and knew that others had greater needs than she did. Another young woman, who had just gone through several trials and had seen God move powerfully in her life, quickly spoke up about praying for "things." God had blessed her financially; she now had better living conditions and the money to go on several mission trips. She spoke powerfully of how God answered her prayers.

"Ask and it will be given to you; seek and you will find; knock and the door will be opened to you. For everyone who asks receives; he who seeks finds; and to him who knocks, the door will be opened." (Matthew 7:7-8)

You do not have, because you do not ask God. When you ask, you do not receive, because you ask with wrong motives, that you may spend what you get on your pleasures. (James 4:2b-3)

People will say things like, "But I pray all the time." James teaches us to pray with the right motives. Too often we are absorbed in ourselves instead of thinking of others. God is not required to answer the prayers that are just for our own comforts or desires. When God answers our prayers, He meets our personal needs and supplies us with what we must have to do His work, and bring glory to His name. The reason God answered the young woman's prayers was because she had the right motives. She had unmet personal needs but she also asked God to bless her above and beyond what she actually needed so she could serve Him on the mission field. God delivered all this and more. The other young woman had a sense of guilt because she had more than other people. God is not concerned with us having too much as long as our hearts are fully devoted to Him. In addition, the reason why we have blessings is to share them with others and build His Kingdom. In fact, God is looking for people on whom He can pour out resources, who, in turn, will dedicate those resources to building His Kingdom.

Praying in Faith

People can make prayer so complicated. If you break it down to its simplest form, answered prayer is simply knowing what God wants to do and asking Him to do it in your life. When we know what God's will is and ask Him to do it, He will. This is why it is so important to know God's Word. His Word is His will. Every time we read the Bible or hear a preacher teaching the Word of God, we learn more about His plan. When we agree with His plan, His power is released, and things happen.

Some people will say that they prayed for something but it didn't happen. We already talked about how God doesn't answer selfish prayers. The other kind of prayer that God does not answer is prayer that is not offered in faith.

"If you believe, you will receive whatever you ask for in prayer." (Matthew 21:22)

Faith is simply believing that God will do what He says He will do. Faith is a trust issue. Either God is God or He's not. Either He is able to do what He says or He is not. We must believe and not doubt, and then He promises we will receive whatever we ask for in prayer when prayed in agreement with His Word and in faith. This can be very difficult at times because we want to solve our own problems and to understand every detail of life. There are times when we must stop trying to figure everything out and just trust God. We have to be like small children who are born with the gift of trust.

"I tell you the truth, anyone who will not receive the kingdom of God like a little child will never enter it." (Mark 10:15)

This does not mean that we just shut off our brains and trust anything. It means acknowledging that God is loving, trustworthy, and dependable at all times. Therefore, as we go through life and don't know how to handle our problems, we admit God knows more than we do, so we put ourselves under His wisdom, knowledge, and way of doing things. This is often when we learn the most about Him. When people doubt, they actually remove themselves from a place of receiving.

But when he asks, he must believe and not doubt, because he who doubts is like a wave of the sea, blown and tossed by the wind. That man should not think he will receive anything from the Lord; he is a double-minded man, unstable in all he does. (James 1:6-8)

Some people say they trust God but spend a lot of time and energy worrying about all kinds of things. You have to make a choice; either you trust Him or you don't. When you trust God, you become stable. Life and emotions are very real. Faith means looking past current realities because you know God already has a different ending to the situation that you are in. It is not denying reality; it's acknowledging that God is bigger than your situation and He's getting ready to bring some much-needed change.

Receiving When Other People Pray for Us

Therefore confess your sins to each other and pray for each other so that you may be healed. The prayer of a righteous man is powerful and effective. (James 5:16)

This Scripture teaches us some powerful truths. When a righteous person prays, those prayers are powerful and effective. The question is, Who is righteous? On our own, no one is righteous. But through the Cross of Jesus Christ, all those who have put their faith and hope in Him have been washed clean of all their sins by His blood. When God looks at us, once we are forgiven and cleansed, He sees us as righteous. Not on our own merit, but simply based on what Jesus did. From that point on, our prayers are powerful and effective. When we sin, we must confess our sin and receive forgiveness. This will allow us to live a life of powerful prayer. Over time, we will sin less and walk in God's power more.

There is power when people pray for us. James tells us there is a healing that takes place through this type of prayer. Our sin is a result of the brokenness in our minds, emotions, and spirit. As our brokenness is healed, we will be changed.

Receiving Prayer Along With the Laying On of Hands

The Bible teaches us that there are times when people should lay hands on the person they are praying for. "Laying on of hands" means the person praying makes physical contact with the one being prayed for by gently placing their hands on the forehead, shoulder, or by holding their hands. This is seen in the life of Jesus and those who followed Him in the New Testament.

Jesus said, "Let the little children come to me, and do not hinder them, for the kingdom of heaven belongs to such as these." When he had placed his hands on them, he went on from there. (Matthew 19:14-15)

There is a spiritual transfer, or impartation, when people lay their hands on someone and pray. (An impartation is when God gives something through the power of His Holy Spirit.) This often happens as God works through people. There is also a principle that when people touch and agree, God answers their prayer.

Therefore let us leave the elementary teachings about Christ and go on to maturity, not laying again the foundation of repentance from acts that lead to death, and of faith in God, instruction about baptisms, the laying on of hands, the resurrection of the dead, and eternal judgment. (Hebrews 6:1-2)

There are groups of Christians who don't practice the spiritual act of laying on of hands. This is a shame because when a righteous person prays and lays hands on the one being prayed for, there is power released through the prayer. The writer of Hebrews teaches us that this is an elementary teaching about Christ, but yet few preachers ever teach on it or utilize it with their congregations. In fact, the writer assumes this basic principle is thoroughly understood by his readers and was eager to move to more important matters. There are many churches that don't practice this type of prayer. There was a holy impartation, or deposit, made when the Church leaders in the New Testament prayed for people, and this is our model to live by. The following are two Scriptures that show how God gave gifts and established leadership roles through prayer, combined with the laying on of hands:

They presented these men to the apostles, who prayed and laid their hands on them. (Acts 6:6)

Do not neglect your gift, which was given you through a prophetic message when the body of elders laid their hands on you. (1 Timothy 4:14)

There are times when people are hesitant to have others pray for them, especially in public settings. My personal experience with people praying for me has been tremendous. Early on in my days of following Christ, I would answer just about any altar call for prayer. This was for two reasons: First, I wanted more of God and what He had for me, and second, I had every problem they were praying about! Much of who I am and what I have accomplished is because of personal ministry received through men and women of God.

I wonder what would have happened if Timothy had not received the prayer and prophetic word that day. Would he have become a great leader in God's Kingdom? Would he have received two personal letters from the Apostle Paul that become books in the Bible? He might have totally missed what God had for him if he hadn't received the prayer and prophetic ministry as a young man. This Scripture teaches us that God gave Timothy a gift through prayer and prophecy. God literally worked through the hands and prayers of men to deposit a gift within him that allowed him to live out the purpose for which God created him.

Healing and Being Set Free

There are also times when God heals people through the laying on of hands.

> *When the sun was setting, the people brought to Jesus all who had various kinds of sickness, and laying his hands on each one, he healed them. Moreover, demons came out of many people, shouting, "You are the Son of God!" But he rebuked them and would not allow them to speak, because they knew he was the Christ. (Luke 4:40-41)*

I have seen this repeatedly. In my own life there was a time, for several years, when I suffered from chronic fatigue. During a church service, the minister asked if anyone wanted to receive prayer for any illness. I went forward and was healed from chronic fatigue that day. When one of my daughters was only a couple of months old, she had a severe fever and the doctor thought she had spinal meningitis. He told us to take her to the emergency room. After prayer, her temperature dropped instantly from 105 degrees to 99 degrees. Nevertheless, we brought her to the hospital to be checked and the doctors were completely baffled. That is the power of prayer. There are times when we must receive healing through prayer.

Receiving Through the Prayers of Jesus

People can be very curious about what actually goes on in Heaven. We don't know all things, but one thing we can be sure of is that Jesus is busy praying for us.

Christ Jesus, who died—more than that, who was raised to life—is at the right hand of God and is also interceding for us. (Romans 8:34)

... but because Jesus lives forever, he has a permanent priesthood. Therefore he is able to save completely those who come to God through him, because he always lives to intercede for them. (Hebrews 7:24-25)

To *intercede* means that Jesus is praying for us. These two Scriptures show us that He is currently bringing requests to God, the Father, on our behalf. When we follow Him, we will receive many blessings because of His prayers on our behalf. In Hebrews it says that Jesus *"lives to intercede for them."* This means that at this time, one of the roles Jesus has is to pray for us. We can also be confident that Jesus only intercedes according to God's will, therefore, we can know that everything He prays for us will happen if we will only believe and receive.

Holy Spirit Helping Us Pray

The reality is that there are times when we don't know the best way or even have the words to pray the right way.

> *In the same way, the Spirit helps us in our weakness. We do not know what we ought to pray for, but the Spirit himself intercedes for us with groans that words cannot express. And he who searches our hearts knows the mind of the Spirit, because the Spirit intercedes for the saints in accordance with God's will.* (Romans 8:26-27)

God is so gracious to us that He helps us to pray in even in our weakness. God's Spirit himself prays for us and through us in ways that our own words cannot express. I thank God that He does not leave us to ourselves and our own insufficiencies. In fact, in our time of weakness, we can experience our greatest prayers. When the Holy Spirit is interceding for us, praying in agreement with the will of God, we can have confidence that God hears our prayers and answers them.

> *This is the confidence we have in approaching God: that if we ask anything according to his will, he hears us. And if we know that he hears us—whatever we*

ask—we know that we have what we asked of him.
(1 John 5:14-15)

As this Scripture teaches, the Holy Spirit helps us pray according to God's will and the result is that our prayer is answered. Praying with the help of the Holy Spirit is one of the keys to receiving the things God has for us.

This chapter is only a brief introduction to our receiving through prayer. If we can just get the basics, we will be on our way. As you grow in your prayer life, remember these basic principles:

- We must personally pray, and these prayers must be offered in faith.

- We must receive through the prayers of others, which at times may include the laying on of hands.

- We must ask the Holy Spirit to fill us and help us pray.

- We should expect great things—even things that we may be unaware of—because Jesus is at the right hand of the Father praying for each of us.

Chapter 8

Receiving from God's Word and His People

Your word is a lamp to my feet and a light for my path. (Psalm 119:105)

God teaches and leads us in several ways. First, through His Word. If it is written in the Bible, it is God's will and you can live by it and depend on it. Next, we must receive from people. God has ordained people whose purpose in life is to equip us to do the work of ministry. (See Ephesians 4:11-12.) We must receive from these people. Their job is to speak what the Father has told them, just as Jesus did.

So whatever I say is just what the Father has told me to say. (John 12:50b)

There are many people who think that they don't need to go to church or to listen to the leaders of the church. First, it is by God's will and authority that the leaders of the Church are established.

Everyone must submit himself to the governing authorities, for there is no authority except that which God has established. The authorities that exist have been established by God. Consequently, he who rebels against the authority is rebelling against what God has instituted, and those who do so will bring judgment on themselves. (Romans 13:1-2)

While this Scripture is referring specifically to governmental authorities, the principle also applies to leaders within the Church. In addition to that, each leader in the Church is there to impart something to us. We will receive what God has for us to the degree that we give our leaders the honor and respect they deserve. We may have to look past the person at times in order to receive what they have to give. This does not mean that we overlook sin or submit to sin; we should never do that. But it does mean that we may have to look past the outside to get what is inside. Even God said that.

"The LORD does not look at the things man looks at. Man looks at the outward appearance, but the LORD looks at the heart." (1 Samuel 16:7)

God deliberately sends people to us to help us mature in our faith through receiving what God has deposited in them.

"He who receives you receives me, and he who receives me receives the one who sent me. Anyone who receives a prophet because he is a prophet

will receive a prophet's reward, and anyone who receives a righteous man because he is a righteous man will receive a righteous man's reward." (Matthew 10:40-41)

God has given gifts to men and women to build up the Body of Christ. We receive benefits from those gifts to the degree that we receive the person with that gift. When a prophet speaks, he speaks God's will to an individual, church, or society as a whole. As we receive it, we receive direction on how to live and influence our world. Even a righteous man, who may not have charisma or a stunning personality that we are attracted to, may have something powerful for us. In fact, he may be rather plain or even boring, but he is righteous and there is a reward for receiving him. By receiving him, it means giving honor, respect, and an open ear. How many people have lost out on a great reward because the preacher didn't shout or speak or sing with great skill in the way that they personally prefer? Even Moses said he was not eloquent (see Exodus 4:10), and the Apostle Paul said that he did not speak with eloquent wisdom. (See 1 Corinthians 1:17, NRSV.)

When it comes to receiving from people, we are sometimes hindered by our own way of looking at life. I have been on both sides of this equation. When I was a new Christian, I had some personal preferences and prejudices that I had to overcome. I had always been involved with sports and working out, so if people were not in great shape or didn't look fit, I was prejudiced against them. However, I found it very easy to receive from people if they presented the image I preferred.

I thank God that He quickly dealt with my wrong thinking. Jesus had so radically changed my life that I took advantage of every prayer meeting and service that I could attend. I just wanted more of God. God confronted me with the truth that when He chooses and empowers someone, they will move in His power. It seemed everywhere I went someone would begin to pray or preach who didn't fit the image that I wanted to see, but my heart would always be touched. These ministers would pray, exhort, or teach with such power that I would begin to weep in God's presence. He taught me to not look at the outside, but on their hearts. I thank God that He helped me receive through all kinds of people even when my heart wasn't in the right place. My desire to receive more of Him overrode my personal prejudices.

There is a danger of missing the things God has for us when we shut out certain people because of who they are. This could mean age, speaking style, culture, ethnicity, gender, denomination, or some other personal preference or prejudice. If we are not careful, our hearts can be hardened, and we can miss what God wants to speak to us through His ambassadors. By this I mean spiritual strengths that God has called to communicate to us through them. Different believers have different anointings. God may send these people to your church or may send you to a conference or other meeting to receive something you need at the time. Be careful not to miss it.

God has given His servants diverse types of gifts. There is no one person who possesses all the gifts, so we have to be ready to receive from a variety of people.

It was he who gave some to be apostles, some to be prophets, some to be evangelists, and some to be pastors and teachers, to prepare God's people for works of service, so that the body of Christ may be built up until we all reach unity in the faith and in the knowledge of the Son of God and become mature, attaining to the whole measure of the fullness of Christ. (Ephesians 4:11-13)

One reason the Body of Christ does not function in unity of power is because of our inability to receive from people different from ourselves. There are many Christians who love their own pastor but will not open their hearts and minds to anyone else. Loyalty to the senior pastor of your church is very important, but the reality is that the senior pastor is only one person with a limited gift. His gift may be tremendous and he may be a great pastor, but he is limited. To receive the fullness of what God has for us, it has to come from a variety of believers. They should not be in conflict with one another; in fact they should complement and add to one another in completing God's work. They will probably have different personalities and styles because of whom God created them to be, so we must stay open-minded. This doesn't mean we compromise God's Word, but we may have to compromise our personal preference on how particular individuals minister.

Not Receiving From Your Own Pastor

A sad reality is that many believers do not receive everything they could from their own pastor. One of the certainties of life is that when we are around people on a regular basis, we begin to take them for granted. How many husbands and wives don't appreciate each other as much as when they were first married? How many people don't appreciate the friends they always spend time with? The same thing happens in our churches. I have observed, even in my own church, that visitors seem to appreciate the pastor more than the people do who are there every week. This results in the visitors getting more out of the service than the members do, even at their own church.

Also, let's not forget the spiritual dynamic that happens when the people in the pews have a greater expectation or level of faith—a greater level of ministry takes place. I have seen and experienced in my own life that when a minister goes to another church, there is more respect and expectation, which results in a more powerful move of God than in their own church. People are excited and have greater faith for God to work when a guest minister is at their church. God answers this faith and does something in their lives. Even Jesus was not given respect in His own hometown, which resulted in fewer miracles, decreased power, and less opportunities for personal ministry than in other towns. Unfortunately, the same thing is still going on. Our senior pastor and associate pastors are gifts from God and we will receive from them in proportion to our faith.

Ministering to Those With Low Expectations

There may be a time when you have the opportunity to share your faith, encourage someone, or even minister in a public setting to people who don't expect much from either you or God. This can be difficult but we must press on if we know God wants His message to be heard. Only God can touch people's hearts and change their minds; we just have to open our mouths and speak forth what He has for us to say.

I have experienced times when I have ministered in other places, and people had low expectations of seeing God at work. This may because they lacked faith, they would rather be listening to someone else, they have already judged me, or they may not expect much from me. My primary ministry is to youth and the young adult generation. Because of this, sometimes people have a low expectation because I "only work with teenagers." Several days after preaching to our adult congregation in my own church, a woman came up to me and said she was blessed by my message. I thanked her for her kind words. Then she looked at me and said, "I didn't think you were that smart." I smiled again and said I was glad that she was blessed by the message. I had another pastor tell me that his people were not ready for my message because they thought I was "only a youth leader." For me, ministering to adults is actually easier—it takes greater gifts to minister to youth. I also choose to minister primarily to youth because that is where God has assigned me and where I believe is the greatest mission field on Earth.

Other times I minister to congregations where I am the only one of my race. This can be very interesting as the people feel me out to see what I have to say. I am completely comfortable in these situations and, in fact, I enjoy these times. As God's Word goes forth, people will forget my age, ethnicity, and primary calling as they open their hearts to what God is speaking to them through me. I encourage you as you share your faith, serve, or minister to people, not to be limited by who you are or what people think of you. God is more powerful than the thoughts of man and if we will hold on for a while, we will see how God can work through us.

It is not as important that people accept us as it is for people to accept our message. We have to do our best to be ourselves and to love people and communicate to them in a way that they can receive. This is true whether we are speaking to people one-on-one or in a group. We must also make sure that we do everything we cannot only communicate clearly, but to not do anything that could possibly be misunderstood or be offensive.

Remember, one of the ways God speaks to us is through people. This means we have to always be ready to receive from others and be ready to share with others in ways that will help them grow closer to the Lord. Always, the first step is receiving. We cannot grow in an area where we have not received. If we want God to use us to change the world, we must first receive. As we grow in our faith, God will teach us to receive more and more. As we receive and grow, we will begin to understand God's authority over all situations.

Section 3

Grow

Chapter 9

Walking in Authority

God has given us greater authority and power than many of us realize. The same power that raised Jesus Christ from the dead lives within every follower of Christ.

And if the Spirit of him who raised Jesus from the dead is living in you, he who raised Christ from the dead will also give life to your mortal bodies through his Spirit, who lives in you. (Romans 8:11)

Don't you know that you yourselves are God's temple and that God's Spirit lives in you? (1 Corinthians 3:16)

That power is actually not a power, but a person—the Holy Spirit. Jesus tells us that anyone who has faith in Him will do the same deeds and works that He did. I like this, because I fall into the "anyone" crowd. It means I can see God move powerfully in and through my life on a regular basis, just as in Jesus' life.

"I tell you the truth, anyone who has faith in me will do what I have been doing. He will do even greater things than these, because I am going to the Father. And I will do whatever you ask in my name, so that the Son may bring glory to the Father. You may ask me for anything in my name, and I will do it." (John 14:12-14)

The Power Is the Holy Spirit

"If you love me, you will obey what I command. And I will ask the Father, and he will give you another Counselor to be with you forever—the Spirit of truth. The world cannot accept him, because it neither sees him nor knows him. But you know him, for he lives with you and will be in you." (John 14:15-17)

When we follow Christ, we receive the Holy Spirit who lives with us and in us. This is where the power, faith, and authority come from. It is not dependent on us or our own strength, but on the power of God. As we gain understanding, our faith grows, and as our faith grows, so will the mighty things that God does through us. God means to work through us to change the world. We are the vessels that God works through. We just have to say "yes" to God. No matter where God sends us or whatever He asks us to do, He will provide everything we need to do what He wants done.

It Is a Matter of Authority

Then Jesus came to them and said, "All authority in heaven and on earth has been given to me. Therefore go and make disciples of all nations, baptizing them in the name of the Father and of the Son and of the Holy Spirit, and teaching them to obey everything I have commanded you. And surely I am with you always, to the very end of the age." (Matthew 28:18-20)

When Jesus says *all*, He means *all*. God the Father gave all authority to Jesus. Jesus then gives us authority to continue the work He began. Few Christians grasp this concept. Very few Christians walk in even a small portion of the authority that God freely gives us. That is why the Church as a whole has not achieved the Great Commission and so many of the evils of this world are still at work. Instead of complaining about problems, God is sending us to overcome and conquer them. The solution to men's problems is not government, education, or anything else devised by man. The solution is the power of God working through people in every situation and every strata of society. Evil triumphs because good people do nothing. Families, towns, cities, and nations are changed when people grab on to authority and walk it out.

As someone who has served in church as a volunteer and on staff, I have observed things from a different perspective. Too many people relegate the power of God only to people in full-time ministry. This should not be. God will work powerfully through anyone who has faith, will take a risk, and expect God to show up. I have lived my Christian life on the edge. I live every day in a place where, if God does not show up, I am in trouble. But the amazing thing is as long as you're where God wants you to be and you are following Him, He always shows up!

The Pastor Is Too Busy

Many people complain that their pastor is too busy. The reason he seems too busy is because he *is* too busy. The average pastor is trying to do too much instead of equipping the congregation to do the work of ministry. The reality is that the problems most people have don't require the attention of the senior pastor. It is also not the job of the senior pastor to babysit everyone in the congregation. The reason the attendance at the average church in America is about seventy people is because this is the maximum number that one person can personally take care of. So instead of building a congregation of people who engage in personal ministry, the pastor spends all of his time, energy, and motivation putting out fire after fire. This needs to change. Average Christians like you and me must begin to understand who they are in Christ and get to work. Most people have problems due to sin and bad choices they themselves have made or because of someone else's actions. These people need relationships, encouragement, love, and correction. This is very time-consuming. This healing should take place primarily through the family, but that is often not the case. The next step should be the support of Christian friends and acquaintances. But the problem is, many Christians are too immature or they don't commit to help others. It takes patient love to help most people.

It is ongoing, often down a bumpy road, but God moves powerfully in these situations.

But I'm Not a Pastor

Don't wait for a title to serve God in a powerful way. Too many people think they are not important to God or they cannot be used powerfully until they are "somebody." Jesus had no title. The apostles had no titles. Many titles are either overused, or, in some cases, even underused. Others are man-made or defined differently from their original intent, and are not prerequisites to do mighty deeds in the name of Jesus. Titles do have their place in the organization of our churches and should be respected, but don't wait until you have one to do the work of ministry. God worked incredibly through my life, using me to lead thousands of people to Him long before I had a title of pastor or minister.

As a new Christian, I simply read the Word of God, believed it, did it, and God always performed what He said He would. I was preaching for several years and leading hundreds of teens to Christ before anyone sat me down to discuss how to write a sermon. I was praying for people and seeing God move powerfully without an understanding of what was happening. It was just natural. I saw people get healed from meningitis, fevers, and cancer without my having an impressive title. God doesn't work through titles, but through people who operate in faith.

But Nobody Respects Me

Welcome to the real world! I work with all age groups, but predominately with teens. It is amazing what little respect many youth pastors and youth leaders get from people. I have consistently had people try to get me to do "real" ministry. It is amazing that 90 percent of people who come to Christ do so before the age of twenty, and so little time, energy, and resources are dedicated to them and the people who serve them. Remember my conversation with the lady in our church who "didn't know I was that smart" after hearing my sermon to the adult congregation? I have learned to never let others get in the way of what God has called me to do. Take a look at what people thought of Jesus:

> While Jesus was still speaking, someone came from the house of Jairus, the synagogue ruler. "Your daughter is dead," he said. "Don't bother the teacher any more."
>
> Hearing this, Jesus said to Jairus, "Don't be afraid; just believe, and she will be healed."
>
> When he arrived at the house of Jairus, he did not let anyone go in with him except Peter, John and James, and the child's father and mother. Meanwhile, all the people were wailing and mourning for her. "Stop wailing," Jesus said. "She is not dead but asleep."
>
> They laughed at him, knowing that she was dead. But he took her by the hand and said, "My child, get up!" Her spirit returned, and at once she stood up. (Luke 8:49-55)

Jesus had just healed a paralyzed man, raised someone from the dead, cast out demons, healed a woman from over a decade of internal bleeding who merely touched the edge of His garment, and people were still mocking and laughing at Him. If people are going to mock and laugh at Jesus, we should not be offended when people don't receive us. I tell people to walk boldly in their faith now and not wait for the approval of man. Jesus did not seek anyone's approval but the Father's, and neither should we.

We are growing and learning about how to receive more from God and walk in greater authority. Receiving is the first step. The next step is growing. It's like giving a boy a baseball bat. He has to learn how to hold it, swing it, and then actually hit the ball. Receiving the bat doesn't guarantee a home run. In fact, it doesn't even guarantee a bunt. Learning, growing, coaching, and practice all come first. All of this is a process. A home run may be in the days ahead, but first comes the process.

Chapter 10

Growth Is a Process

Growth takes time. It is a process that we can influence, but it still takes time. This is difficult for us because we live in an instant society. We expect our fast food immediately. We can microwave anything and we don't ever stand in lines. A few years back I was at a White Castle before a speaking engagement and when I ordered my food they told me to wait in the back and they would call me when it was ready. I actually got aggravated that I had to wait three minutes. We have been conditioned to get what we want immediately, but unfortunately, God does not work that way. God is more concerned with the end result than how long it takes. He sets the clock and He causes the change, but we have to walk out the process.

Embracing the Process

You can't just nuke your faith for sixty seconds and be a spiritual giant. If we are serious about growing and becoming a spiritual powerhouse, we have to embrace the process. The reality is, at times, the process may not be too exciting. It's like a runner who has to go to practice every day and work out. Those workouts are usually tedious, too long, and even painful, but that's the process. What makes a champion runner is not the fact that training was fun, but that the champion embraced the process all the way to greatness. Spiritual champions are built in much the same way.

All Spiritual Growth Begins With a Seed

God always begins with a small seed of His Word. Everything we receive from God is like a seed:

> *He also said, "This is what the kingdom of God is like. A man scatters seed on the ground. Night and day, whether he sleeps or gets up, the seed sprouts and grows, though he does not know how. All by itself the soil produces grain—first the stalk, then the head, then the full kernel in the head. As soon as the grain is ripe, he puts the sickle to it, because the harvest has come."* (Mark 4:26-29)

God is always giving us seed. It comes when we read His Word, hear His Word, and also through Him speaking to us as we pray to Him and live our daily lives. This parable teaches us how the seed grows—first the stalk, then the head, and then the kernel in the head. This involves time, several steps, and finally the fruit. This story says that the farmer doesn't know how it grows. He knows what he must do to make it grow, but he doesn't know how it actually happens. This is because it is God himself who causes the growth. It's a miracle and it can't be fully explained. I personally enjoy this because it lets me know that in order to grow I don't have to understand everything that's going on. I just have to walk out the process.

Protecting the Seed and Letting It Grow

While this growth is taking place, the devil and our own flesh often try to stop the process. The average Christ-follower does not suffer from inadequate seed in his or her life, but inadequate growth. One of the reasons for this is that until there is ripe fruit, we don't see the benefit. Since we don't see it, we often don't think it is coming or we are too impatient to wait for it.

When the seed of God's Word is planted, the devil immediately tries to steal it. If we are immature, that seed may quickly grow—or quickly dry up. Allowing the cares of the world to become our focus and overpower the presence of the Word is another way seed will not grow. The issues of life become our priority instead of God's Word and His will. But if we walk by faith and not by what we see, God's Word will begin to transform us. We have to be okay with the fact there may be several stages we must go through before we actually see real change. I have known many people whom God has changed. He has changed the way they think, the way they react, and the way they talk. They stopped cursing, complaining, whining, and even being sarcastic. While these changes are going on, you might still hear some inappropriate words and see some bad attitudes. This doesn't mean that growth and change haven't occurred; you just haven't given them a chance to mature.

It's Not About a Feeling

One of our greatest struggles is living by our feelings. If we want to be spiritual champions, we must be committed to growth no matter how we feel. The problem with this is that feelings are not always dependable and can get us into trouble when we allow them to set the direction for our lives. In fact, Romans 8:14 gives us specific directions on living by the guidance of the Holy Spirit. This means not living by our feelings, emotions, or the situations we are in. God is bigger than them all.

> *... because those who are led by the Spirit of God are sons of God.* (Romans 8:14)

Proof of us being *"sons of God"* is that we are led by His Spirit in an ever-increasing way. This means we leave behind immaturity and the sin that goes with it. With the power of sin being removed from our lives more and more, our spirit then becomes open to the power of God. He leads us as we follow Him with greater sensitivity and obedience. The word *sons* in this Scripture is not reserved for males, but more appropriately describes people who are maturing in their faith and being continually led. This may be accompanied by good feelings or no feelings at all. It is most important to be led by the Holy Spirit whether or not we are feeling bad or confused. God will always lead us on the right path. It is up to us to be led where God wants to take us even if we feel nothing or have negative emotions.

We Grow From Our Connection

Jesus describes the relationship of the vine and the branches in John 15. He talks about the vine being the source of nourishment that causes the branches to grow and eventually produce fruit. A good vine always produces good fruit. When we stay connected to Jesus, we will always produce good fruit. The key is staying connected. Sometimes children get impatient when they plant something and it doesn't grow quickly enough. They pull it out of the ground to see if the roots are okay and in the process they either shock or kill the plant and it never produces fruit.

Growth Is a Journey

Since we live in a fast-food, microwave society, we want results immediately. We have been conditioned not to wait for anything. It's all about instant gratification. Honestly, I enjoy the ability to microwave a meal or to go to the drive-through and have my food in less than two minutes. The only problem is that God does not work that way. Yes, there are times when God does something in an instant and I love it when He does. But more often, God takes us through a journey. God is more concerned about the result than our feelings. He is in the process of transforming us into the image of His Son. I have found in my life, if, in my opinion, God is taking too long, the problem is not God—it's me.

Ongoing Connection = Ongoing Growth

I believe God would actually do things more quickly if we got with His program instead of us trying to get Him to go along with ours. The reality is, we have to go through a spiritual transformation process. The more we embrace His course of action, the quicker and less painful it will be. Notice I said "less painful," not "pain-free." Change and growth are often painful. They just are. We like comfort and routine, but remember God is more concerned about the end result. When we focus on becoming more like Christ, that result is always better and, although it may be uncomfortable at times along the way, the trip will be much better, too.

God Gives Us Seed Potential

God not only created us with great potential, He is constantly adding potential to our lives through His Word. When we receive His Word, it is not a finished product. It is a seed.

What is more valuable, an apple or the seeds within the apple? While the apple looks better, tastes better, and gives us immediate results and satisfaction, the seeds have much more potential. When we eat an apple, we gain the benefits of good taste and a little energy, but a few hours later we could be hungry again. However, we won't have the apple to satisfy that hunger because we've already eaten it.

The seeds inside the apple are small and don't look like very much, but they really have much more potential. If you took those seeds and planted them, each one could produce an entire tree and bear thousands of apples before it was done. Each seed within those apples could do the same. If you had enough time, you could literally grow an entire apple orchard from one apple seed.

God's Word is like that. One seed will begin to grow and multiply in your life. The more seeds, the faster and better the growth. Within God's Word is an endless supply of seed that will grow and touch every part of your life, if you have the patience to let it happen.

Growth Comes in Stages

One of the keys to letting a plant grow is to protect it and give it time to grow. The growth always goes downward into the ground before it comes up. Without strong roots, no plant can live. It takes about ten years for an apple tree to produce apples. Long before that, the roots are going down and spreading out to get water and nutrients. The tree has to grow strong to support the weight of leaves and fruit. This also takes time. Pulling the tree out of the ground to look at the roots is the best way to guarantee no fruit. It is the same with Christ-followers; we have to keep our eyes on God and not ourselves, stay connected with the Church, be constantly filled with God's Word, and give ourselves time to grow.

"Night and day, whether he sleeps or gets up, the seed sprouts and grows, though he does not know how." (Mark 4:27)

At first glance, this doesn't seem very exciting. Every night you go to sleep and get up the next day. Growth is taking place, but we don't know how. There are definitely things we need to do to grow spiritually, but some of the growth happens and we don't know how. Just like plants grow from sun and rain, we grow from God's Word and His presence in our lives. We understand parts of it, but not all of it. Even when we don't understand everything, we are still growing. God is a miraculous God who is always at work. I thank God that He is constantly changing and growing us even when we do not know how He is doing it.

Walking Out the Process

"All by itself the soil produces grain—first the stalk, then the head, then the full kernel in the head." (Mark 4:28)

There are times when God supernaturally delivers us from sin, sickness, bad habits, fear, and many other things. God may take a drug dealer and quickly turn him into a preacher, but this is very rare. In my experience, this usually happens in stages. This Scripture is talking about grain growing. First comes the stalk. This is a rather unimpressive-looking plant that obviously can't be eaten. There are times when people are overcoming habits or behaviors that they have had for years. There is a level of growth taking place, but the behavior is still present. It is exhibited less often and it's not as strong, but it's still there. I have heard people say: "I'm not where I want to be, but I'm not where I used to be!" Of course, this can be an excuse people make, but honestly it is a statement that we can all say about some area of our lives. The key to overcoming sin or fear is continued growth. It may not look like much to us and to those around us, but if there is ongoing growth, there will be victory. Others are discovering their gifts and gradually learning to walk in them. The greater the transformation to Christ-likeness, the greater the ministry will be.

The head of the grain comes next. This is when we are starting to see change and God's power working and things are starting to look better. It's not fruit yet, but it's on its way. Once again, it is important to let the growth continue so we can see the full-grown kernels of wheat. Spiritually, this is often when people get comfortable; they have seen change and growth and feel like it is enough. They may do a few things for God, be satisfied, and not believe for anything more. The problem is they aren't full-grown, ripe, spiritual fruit yet. It's like running almost twenty-six miles in a marathon and then stopping a couple of hundred feet before the finish line. No one would do that naturally, but many people do that spiritually.

Ripe Fruit = Victory

Whether it's winning someone to Christ, overcoming sin, receiving healing physically or emotionally, our goal is to finish and see the full-grown fruit through the power of God. When that kernel is full, the farmer puts the sickle to it and it is harvest time. We must live a life where once God has done what He wants to do, the growth has taken place, and the victory has been won, we take hold of that victory and continue to walk in it.

But I Don't Feel Like I Am Growing

Growth does not depend on how you feel. There are times when growth is exciting and noticeable; other times it is happening, but we can't really sense it. It's like seeing a child that you haven't been around for a year. That child has grown a couple of inches and you can notice the difference, but the child may not. If you asked them if they felt their body or hair grow each day, they would probably look at you strangely. They didn't *feel* their body or hair grow, but it sure did. Every day they ate food, slept, and grew. Spiritually, we must read God's Word, pray, worship, and serve, and we will grow. We may not notice the difference on a daily basis, but it will be clear to both us and to those around us. Don't focus on the feeling; focus on doing the things that will cause growth.

Growth Helps Us Overcome

Oh, how I love the promises of Jesus, except one. In John 16:33 Jesus lets us know that in our lives we will have trouble. But thank God, that is not the end of the story.

> *"I have told you these things, so that in me you may have peace. In this world you will have trouble. But take heart! I have overcome the world."* (John 16:33)

First, Jesus lets us know that the things He has told us will give us peace. This is a tremendous advantage that followers of Christ have that those who don't follow Christ don't have. Before I began my relationship with

Jesus, I accomplished and experienced most of the things that I desired, but I never had peace. After working through some issues as a new Christian, I soon had great peace for the first time in my life. But even with peace, whether we like it or not, trouble will come. Then Jesus tells us not to worry because He has overcome the world. The term *world* means the physical world and its system of how things function. And in this world's system, we will have trouble. But since Jesus overcame the world, as His followers so should we.

Staying on the Course of God's Grace

We have to walk the path of growth. Growth is not a prayer away; it takes time and doing the things on purpose that foster growth. God, through His grace, gives us everything we need in seed form that will grow over time if we water and fertilize it.

> *But grow in the grace and knowledge of our Lord and Savior Jesus Christ. To him be glory both now and forever! Amen.* (2 Peter 3:18)

Too many people think that receiving God's forgiveness and grace is like crossing the finish line. It is not the finish line; in fact, it's the starting line. There is also a type of knowledge we gain about Jesus. It is about getting to know Jesus in detail and in depth. If we want to grow to be more like Him, we must know Him intimately. This brings power into our lives and brings glory to Him. We can do this in many ways, but two of the most important are through His Word and through the people He has chosen to teach and train us.

Grace can mean a couple of different things. The first meaning of grace is we are forgiven even though we don't deserve it. It is an expression of God's mercy and love that allows us to be set free from past sin and poor judgment. Another type of grace is God releasing His power on us and through us to do what He has created us to do. So grace not only sets us free, but also gives us the power to do the same things Jesus did and even greater things (see John 14:12). Both are a demonstration in our lives of doing things that we could not do on our own. As we grow in this grace, we grow in God's power and ability to love, forgive, change, and to perform mighty deeds through His power. This is also how God brings glory to himself. When people see great things done through ordinary people like us, they wonder how it is possible. We then have an opportunity to tell them about the greatness of God.

Growing Through God's Word

One of the greatest ways to learn about God's grace and gain knowledge of Him is through His written Word. If we want to have knowledge of Jesus, we must get to know His Word. John 1:1 says: *"In the beginning was the Word, and the Word was with God, and the Word was God."* A few verses later in verse 14, it says: *"The Word became flesh and made his dwelling among us."*

Basically, God's Word is a written expression of Jesus Christ. Through all of the history, prophecy, poetry, letters and gospels written in the Bible, we learn about Jesus. The

Bible shows how God has interacted with mankind since He created us. It teaches us the character, personality, and ways of Jesus Christ and can lead us through the turbulent waters of life. Jesus calls himself the light of the world (see John 8:12) and David also writes that God's Word is a light to our path. They both show us how to go through life.

So as we go through the many twists and turns of life, God will show us the way. *"Your word is a lamp to my feet and a light for my path"* (Psalm 119:105). This was written in a day when there was no electricity and walking outside in the dark could be a dangerous activity. So for people to see where they were going, they would hang a lantern on the end of a long pole and hold it in front of their feet. It only let them see a few paces ahead, but they knew they were safe at least for the next couple of steps.

Trusting God One Step at a Time

We want God to show us everything He has planned for our lives right now. For many people, they are ready to trust God after He shows them their career, future spouse, the house they will live in, and the answers to all their other questions. After God shows them and guarantees all of these things, then they will put their trust in Him. But God does not work that way. He wants us to walk by faith and trust Him step by step. Even though the lantern only gives light to one or two steps ahead, something amazing happens each time you take a step and move forward. The lantern moves forward also, allowing you to take another step until you get to your destination. God's Word works the same way, as we continue to follow Jesus. With each step, we can see a step farther and progress to our destination. As we continue to see step by step, another amazing thing happens: God's Word also begins to light our path. Our path is more than just a few steps; it is the road we are to travel. So as each step is given light, our path becomes brighter. Before we know it, we have reached another great destination God has prepared for us, and we got there step by step.

Allowing God's Word to Unfold in Your Life

One of the dangers and struggles we face is being tempted to jump off the path and not follow Jesus step by step. The cares of the world and the busyness of life can very easily pull us away from God's path. One of the main reasons for this is impatience. We must embrace the growth process and let it happen gradually. Just like growing taller or growing our hair longer will take time, so will spiritual growth. Picture God's Word as a map in your life. Like a map must be taken out of the glove compartment and unfolded to be useful, God's Word to you must be unfolded from the pages of the Bible.

The unfolding of your words gives light; it gives understanding to the simple. (Psalm 119:130)

Remember, if we want to understand God's Word and walk in greater power and authority, we will have to overcome our instant gratification mind-set. We have been trained by our culture to expect instant results. This can cause us to expect God to work in the way we want Him to work. For many people, if God doesn't work according to their timeline and expectation, they decide God is either not real or not worth the wait. We want the light, but we want it when we want and how we want it. Many people walk away from God or shift their focus back to self-reliance because they are impatient.

The light, or direction, comes from God's Word, but it unfolds over time. God's Word teaches us that God speaks to us and directs us. I have spoken to people who say: "God doesn't speak to me." God does speak to us; the question is: Do we listen and obey? The speaking is on His terms, not ours. Many people don't hear what God is saying both directly and through His Word because they are impatient and won't let it unfold. There have been Scriptures I have read many times but on one particular day, they mean more than ever before. On that day, God unfolded a greater understanding to me because I was faithful. Keep reading God's Word and trust it. God will unfold it to you in greater ways as the days go by.

Understanding God's Word

This verse also says that God's Word gives understanding to the simple. People too often read the Bible, come across something they don't yet comprehend, and claim: "The Bible is too hard to understand." This statement is just not true. God would not give us a book that we could not understand. His Word will help you understand life. When the Bible uses the word *simple*, it is not a nice word. *Simpleton* is an old word that we don't use anymore and it basically means an ignorant, stupid person. God is telling us that we don't need a Ph.D. or another type of degree to understand His Word. This is good because anyone can qualify when it comes to understanding His Word.

If you are reading this book and have gotten this far, you would not be considered "simple." That means that you are able to understand God's Word. Don't believe the lie of the devil that you can't understand it. Ask God to teach you and show you and He will.

The Purpose of Receiving From People

Earlier in the book we talked about receiving from people. Specifically, we looked at the role of the fivefold ministry: apostles, prophets, evangelists, pastors, and teachers set forth in Ephesians 4:11. As these gifted people pour themselves into our lives, we are prepared to do the work of service and become mature. As we mature, we grow to be more like Christ.

> *... until we all reach unity in the faith and in the knowledge of the Son of God and become mature, attaining to the whole measure of the fullness of Christ. Then we will no longer be infants, tossed back and forth by the waves, and blown here and there by every wind of teaching and by the cunning and craftiness of men in their deceitful scheming. Instead, speaking the truth in love, we will in all things grow up into him who is the Head, that is, Christ. (Ephesians 4:13-15)*

Too often we want to overcome life's challenges in our own strength or wisdom and it doesn't work. Only when we grow up to be like Christ do we also gain the strength to overcome the world. The purpose of receiving from God's leaders is to bring us to this point. We need leaders and we need each other. You may be moving full steam ahead in God's purposes or you may be far away from this reality.

Just Take a Step

Many people feel unworthy or that they have too far to go to become like Jesus. One of the things I love about Jesus is that He accepts us as we are. You can come to Him in any condition and He will love you and receive you. He will also begin to change you. Jesus changes you not to accept or love you more, but to make it possible for you to live out the great life He created you to live. Too many people think the beginning a relationship is the finish line. They figure they are forgiven, they will go to Heaven, and that takes care of that, so let's get on with the rest of life. Following Christ *is* your life! Doing His works is your destiny and purpose in life. Receiving Jesus as Lord and Savior is only the beginning of the greatest adventure you could ever live. Salvation is only the beginning.

> *Like newborn babies, crave pure spiritual milk, so that by it you may grow up in your salvation, now that you have tasted that the Lord is good.* (1 Peter 2:2-3)

God's Word is teaching us that we must grow up in our salvation. It is not only an experience, but also a growth process. As we mature in our faith, salvation becomes more real. It begins to affect every aspect of our lives. Our thinking, emotions, actions, and outlook change to become more Christ-like. We begin to view the world as Christ does. We learn to love and forgive and to walk in the authority that brings change wherever we go. But first we have to grow up. We grow faster when we are surrounded by others who are also growing and encouraging us along the way.

Chapter 11

Growth Occurs Best in Community

We need community. God created us in such a way that makes us desire to be part of a group of people. That's why people stay in certain places or move to others. People join teams, clubs, associations, and even gangs in the search of community. We all have different levels of need and wanting to belong, but just about everybody desires to be connected with other people. I would go so far as to say that it is abnormal to want to be alone all the time. We need peace and quiet to unwind and this is good, but a lack of connection is actually bad for us. Isolation is detrimental to people physically, emotionally, psychologically, and spiritually.

No matter where you go in the world, people organize themselves into communities. On the big level, we have towns, cities, states, provinces, and countries. Inside, we know that we need to be part of something and that we benefit by being connected to others. Even people who adopt lifestyles, habits, or ways that are completely different from what is considered normal, end up being connected with people who are very much like them. I recently received an email from some people with extreme tattoos and body piercings. Each of these people made a decision to be different from the norm. In each of the pictures, these "extreme" and "different" people were surrounded by people who looked just like them. It is funny how all kinds of "different" people group together in a community.

The reality is that God created us with a need to be around other people. People who spend time with each other begin to act and even look alike, and by doing so, they have just created their own little community. Since God created us, He knows that we live the best kind of life when we are connected to others. I have heard people who claim to be followers of Christ say they don't need to go to church or be connected to other believers. The problem with this type of thinking is that it goes against the lifestyle of Jesus, the teachings of Jesus, and God's Word as a whole. I often ask people the question, "Why did Jesus choose His followers?" People give various reasons, the most common being: because He wanted people to do ministry or to teach them. These may be part of the picture, but it is best shown in the following Scripture:

He appointed twelve—designating them apostles— that they might be with him and that he might send them out to preach. (Mark 3:14)

Jesus was not just choosing people, but choosing people to be with Him. Jesus created a small community. Within this small community, ordinary men became great apostles. A small group of men with very little education, no credentials, and actually quite a few faults, became mighty men of God who changed the world. In the same way today, God wants us to be involved in relationships with individuals and groups of people because change must be demonstrated in connection with other people.

Through these relationships Jesus knew that people would be changed and transformed. Something happens in community that cannot happen in any other situation. You can't get it from a book or personal prayer or personal Bible study. Much of our faith and beliefs can only be seen or experienced in relationships. Here is a partial list of Scriptures that use the words *one another*:

"Love one another." (John 13:34)

Live in harmony with one another. (Romans 12:16)

Accept one another. (Romans 15:7)

… instruct one another. (Romans 15:14)

… agree with one another. (1 Corinthians 1:10)

… serve one another in love. (Galatians 5:13)

… be patient, bearing with one another in love. (Ephesians 4:2)

Be kind and compassionate to one another. (Ephesians 4:32)

Speak to one another with psalms, hymns and spiritual songs. Submit to one another out of reverence for Christ. (Ephesians 5:19; 21)

... admonish one another with all wisdom. (Colossians 3:16)

Therefore encourage one another. (1 Thessalonians 5:11)

But encourage one another daily. (Hebrews 3:13).

... spur one another on toward love and good deeds. (Hebrews 10:24)

... live in harmony with one another. (1 Peter 3:8)

Offer hospitality to one another without grumbling. (1 Peter 4:9)

... have fellowship with one another. (1 John 1:7)

Love, acceptance, encouragement, admonishment, fellowship, and all the others listed above can't be done alone. Can you imagine a person sitting in the corner facing a wall and someone asks them, "What are you doing?" and they tell you, "I'm loving everyone in the world." You would think they were crazy. God's Word teaches us not to just hear the Word, but to do the Word (see James 1:22). This requires relationship, and relationship requires community. It requires that we submit ourselves to God and to each other.

In addition to promoting common values and beliefs, community acts like a pressure cooker. It applies the pressure that seals in the good flavor while heating and burning up things that are displeasing to God. Community requires commitment and that results in maturity over the long haul.

One of the greatest tricks of the devil is to pull us away from the people of God. He knows that we grow best in communities and can be tripped up easiest when we are alone, lonely, or with people who will pull us further away from God.

> *Let us not give up meeting together, as some are in the habit of doing, but let us encourage one another—and all the more as you see the Day approaching.* (Hebrews 10:25)

As we continue to meet together, we are a great source of encouragement to each other. The more time we spend together, the more we can support each other. We all want to do the right thing, but this goes against what the world is doing. We are all influenced by cultural norms. Unless we deliberately do things differently, we will naturally do the things that "everyone else is doing." But when we spend time with people who have higher standards, a different type of norm is established within that group and we then tend to do what that group is doing. This gives us an atmosphere in which to support the convictions and choices we have made to follow God.

Communities Support Common Beliefs and Goals

As we walk out our faith, trials and tribulations come. Temptations, confusion, and fear can take hold of us if we are not careful. There may also be times when we are weak or just tired. Times like these make community so important. I had two young men in my ministry; one of them was serving God, the other wasn't. The godly young man invited his friend to church, and he gave his life to Jesus. They were best friends and they began to serve God together. Then trials came and the young man who was already serving God began to drift away. The other young man—the new Christian—was actually the stronger one. He hung in there and helped his friend come back to God. A year or two later, the situation was reversed and the favor was returned. Then, both young men were serving God because of their friendship and because of the community of believers that surrounded them both. How many people fall away from God because they weren't strongly connected? There are times when we need encouragement and even confrontation to stay on the right road.

In a community, we begin to feel a purpose that is bigger than ourselves. We start to buy in to the vision for the community, we are encouraged to work toward that vision, and the work is shared as we strive to do the work of Christ. The most transformational ministry that I have seen is our Teen Dance ministry. These wonderful young men and women have changed before my eyes over the years. This has all happened because they have formed a small community that meets together every Saturday for several hours. They work, sweat, laugh, cry, and hang out together. There are even times when they get mad, fight, and have to work things out. But this is real life and real community, and this is where real change takes place. Sometimes it happens slowly and it's not easy, but it's worth it. I have seen others come and go in this ministry, but with no lasting change. You could see the beginnings of change, but when the commitment and connection was cut, the growth and change were lost as they returned to former relationships.

In this small dance community, one of the values is not speaking negatively. I have heard people joke because there are members of the team who refuse to complain, whine, or talk badly about other people. They even hold each other accountable to speak life and not death. Others think it is funny or extreme, but it is a value they have been taught and it is something for which they hold each other accountable. This is how community causes you to grow.

Confrontation Occurs in Community

Confrontation is one of the things that causes us to grow and change. In life we are confronted with situations that require us to grow in order to overcome problems or adverse circumstances. Community has a way of keeping us responsible for our actions and for behaving in the right way. I have worked in public schools where all the teachers and students knew each other. I have worked in other schools that were larger and teachers and students didn't know each other well. The behaviors were much different. People act differently when they recognize that others know who they are. Many people will do the wrong thing if they think they can get away with it. I used to make sure that I knew as many kids' names as possible. Students would do things they knew were wrong and then scatter when a teacher came on the scene. I made sure I knew the names of most of the students and especially the ones who were the troublemakers. When I saw them, I would say hello or call them by name. If someone did something wrong, I called them out by name.

It's amazing how people react when they realize that others know who they are. Community has a way of reminding us how important our words and actions are. Everything we do affects the people we are connected to, and we are responsible for both the good and the bad choices we make.

Like having a training partner in athletics or being on a team that is working together, a church community allows us, and, at times, forces us to do things we would never do on our own. When I first became a Christian, our pastor would ask the entire church to fast and pray at certain times. I would have never done that if I were not part of the church. My faith grew quickly and it helped me see many miracles and many lives transformed.

Section 4

Give
It Away

Chapter 12

Mature People Are Givers

We focused first on becoming great receivers. Then we talked about growing in the things that we have received. Now is the time to grow as a giver. As we learn to become greater givers, an interesting thing happens: God continues to give us even more. The more we give away, the more we receive. Immature people try to hold on to what they have instead of being a blessing to others.

It takes maturity to be a giver. Giving first means that you have something. It also means that you are comfortable with giving it away. True giving is sacrificial; it means giving away things that matter to us. It takes maturity to give away things of value. Time, energy, and possessions are all important to us. When it came time for David to make a sacrifice after he had sinned in God's sight, he was given the wood and animals to sacrifice, but he refused to receive them as a gift. He demanded that he pay for them as he boldly declared: *"I will not sacrifice to the LORD my God burnt offerings that cost me nothing"* (2 Samuel 24:24). We need to be able to give at all times and in all situations. This may sound demanding, but that is what Christ did and He is our model.

Immature people are only concerned about themselves. What's in it for them? How can they get what they want or need? They are continually focused on self. All of us are immature at some time and in some areas of our lives. That's why our Christian walk starts out with receiving. It is amazing how much God gives to immature people. I have seen people who are immature spiritually ask God for things and He quickly answers their prayers. Sometimes they don't know how to pray or they pray crazy prayers, but God in His grace rewards those who earnestly seek Him, even when they don't have it all together. One of the reasons God does this is to demonstrate how much of a giver He is. He is also teaching us how to be givers ourselves. We serve a giver-God, so we should be giver-Christians.

Maturity Is Not Necessarily Age-Related

When it comes to giving, spiritual maturity is much more significant than a person's age. Age and maturity should be related, and as we grow older, we should also progress spiritually. This, however, is not always the case. I have seen many young people who were tremendous givers far beyond what would be expected for their age. They had received so much from God that they became givers to their generation. The first person to ever personally attempt to share Christ with me was a fourteen-year-old freshman at a high school where I taught. She was the leader of the high school's Bible club. I walked in to check it out and she boldly shared "The Father's Love Letter" with me. (This is a list of Scriptures put together to explain God's love for us.) She took a risk and she gave. I didn't understand it at the time, but started going to church a few months later and gave my life to Christ that summer. She played an important role in the chain of events that led to my salvation because she didn't wait to give until she was a certain age.

We recently had some friends over for dinner. They brought their one-year-old daughter with them who was becoming friends with my one-year-old daughter. Many children have their special stuffed animal or some other toy they cling to. Our daughter has "Blanky." She loves Blanky, which happens to be light pink and very easy to cuddle with. We were watching the children play and she picked up Blanky and walked over to her friend. When she got to her, she handed her Blanky and said, "Here you go." My wife and I looked at each other in amazement as she received Blanky. Even at only a year, our daughter understands the value of giving something to someone else. She knows that Blanky brings her much happiness, and she was mature enough to recognize that it would bring her friend happiness also; so she gave it to her.

Giving Is Part of Who We Are

The story above demonstrates that God has wired us to be givers. Our baby daughter has older sisters who are also givers, so she has seen others giving. But I believe it was just natural for her to share one of the most important things she has with her friend because she wanted to bless her. Giving makes us feel good. It often amazes me that some of the most generous people are those who have the least. Those who live in lack are often the first ones to give when there is a need. I believe they have learned to live without and realize things don't make you happy. Therefore, things don't have a hold on their lives. They have learned to live without, so they have learned to give even when they don't have the things they need. This shows maturity.

There are also many adults in our churches who are not givers. Some of them have been going to church for decades, but they have not sacrificed and given their time, energy, and resources totally to God. Because of this they have not grown, and people have not been reached with the power of God's love. Stingy people hurt our churches and our society. One of my favorite pastors always said, "Let your life be a donation." We will not see the power of God in our lives until we stop "tipping" God and throwing our leftovers to people in need. We must continually ask God to help us be greater givers and to trust Him to supply us with more to give.

The Cost of Giving

One of the reasons it takes maturity to be a giver is because giving costs. Since God gives us our days to live, our gifts, our talents, and our finances, we should use them for His purposes first. This is hard for many people to see, but when we learn to be givers, we learn to live like our heavenly Father.

Over the years, I have ministered to all age groups, but have focused on teens. One of the biggest reasons that many churches don't have great youth ministries is because youth ministry costs. It costs time that is often directed toward unappreciative people. It costs energy as we try to keep up with their activities and emotions, and it costs money because most of them don't have much. It takes maturity on behalf of church leadership and the congregation to promote and back ministry to youth. Too many people complain about teens and the direction teens are headed, but they are not willing to put their time and money where their mouths are. Ninety percent of people who come to Christ do so by the age of twenty, but very little time and fewer resources of our churches are dedicated to this age group. One of the results of this is many church congregations are shrinking and getting older. It takes maturity to sow seeds that may not produce fruit for years to come. Many churches did not sow into their own youth over the past decades and are paying for it now.

Giving Represents God to the World

Jesus taught much about giving. He taught that giving was a way to change the world. Giving is a demonstration of generosity and even mercy. Jesus even taught that we should give to people who don't deserve it. In the time of Jesus, Israel was ruled by Rome. Under the law, a Roman soldier could force a Jew to carry something for him for one mile. When confronting such injustices, Jesus told people that if they are asked to carry something one mile, they should carry it two (see Matthew 5:41). The principle behind this is when you give, by going above and beyond what is expected, you get people's attention. Every day we have opportunities to do uncommon things for people. We are called to be witnesses and ambassadors for Jesus. That means we actually demonstrate His character and represent Him wherever we go. Giving gets people's attention and when we get people's attention, we are able to point them to God. This brings glory to God and also allows us to share the love of Christ.

Chapter 13

Focusing on People Outside the Church

The needs of people outside the Church are greater than the needs of those inside the Church. I am about to make some pretty big assumptions, but here goes. First, the people in our churches should already know Jesus as Lord and Savior. This means they are connected to the one who will guide them to everything they need in life. We have discussed in detail why people must receive and grow. The next step is giving, because we have what others need. Too many individual Christians—and even entire churches—are so focused on personal or church needs they either don't care or are too busy to focus on people outside the church. Yes, we should help and build up our church members, but at some point we need to focus on those who don't know Jesus. And, yes, we can do both if everyone is actively engaged in personally ministering to others. Throughout our own personal journeys as we minister to others, others will minister to us in times of need. As we mature, we should become less and less needy and focus more on others, especially those who don't yet know Jesus as Lord and Savior.

> *"For the Son of Man came to seek and to save what was lost."* (Luke 19:10)

As followers of Jesus, we are to do the things He did. If Jesus focused on the lost, so should we.

Focusing on the Sick

> *Jesus answered them, "It is not the healthy who need a doctor, but the sick. I have not come to call the righteous, but sinners to repentance."* (Luke 5:31-32)

Focusing on Those Infected With Sin Sickness

The Church should be the greatest organized agent of change on the planet. The Church should be the biggest influence, agent of reform, and trendsetter in existence. This is a far cry from reality in our day and age. In a sermon entitled, "A Church That Matters," I ask the following question: "If your church shut down tomorrow, would it matter?" The reality is that instead of being a beacon of hope and strength to our culture, there are probably thousands of churches that could disappear tomorrow and it wouldn't really matter to the communities they serve. This is sad, but true. The reason some churches could shut down without any great consequence is because, first, they are not affecting individuals and communities in a significant way. Second, other churches are solid churches for their members, but that ends at the church doors. God wants to take these churches to the next level.

Both of these scenarios describe believers who are not focused on the community and people outside their church. When the focus shifts off of self and those already in our churches, we begin to walk in the path of Jesus. Sin sickness is both damaging now and eternally destructive. Ungodly attitudes, lifestyles, and convictions then begin to infect our education, government, entertainment, and business fields. This results in injustice, corruption, and the promotion of sin. As we reach individuals and help them to overcome sin in their lives, these larger systems will also be affected.

Righteous Through the Blood of Jesus— Curing Sin Sickness

Sick people need Dr. Jesus and we need to make house calls. I actually heard of a pastor who said that all they had to do was open the church doors and God would send the people. He didn't want to run programs or events to attract anyone and didn't train his congregation to go and minister to the community. The last I heard, the church continued to shrink and slowly die out. Seek and save—that is what Jesus did. He didn't sit around and hope. As we live in a society that has grown cold toward God, and even against the things of God, churches that want to be relevant and healthy must be *sending* churches. We must be sending fired-up believers into our businesses, government offices, and schools to those who need healing from sin sickness.

The only way people can think, speak, and act right is if God makes them righteous through the blood of Jesus. As our society has grown more ungodly, the prisons are larger; divorce is commonplace; illegal drugs are pervasive in our schools; psychologists and psychiatrists are doing thriving business; and self-help and advice shows have overrun the media. People recognize that they are broken; but not that Jesus alone can make them whole.

Helping Change the Direction of People's Lives

Repentance in its simplest form is simply changing direction. If you are driving east but need to go west, it is time for a U-turn. Many people are in need of a spiritual U-turn. They need to turn away from running their own lives and choosing sin, to turn toward choosing to follow Jesus and living a better way. Our society has deteriorated in its behavior and conduct as people have turned away from faith. This has happened individual by individual and family by family. We can only turn people around and back to Jesus one at a time and family by family. The reality is that this will not be done in our churches, as much as in our homes. People may make public decisions to follow Christ in our churches, but the choices will oftentimes begin in our homes, schools, and workplaces. The process may end with a pastor, but will probably begin in a casual conversation over a cup of coffee or a walk through the mall. We are to be salt and light in the world, not just in church.

Givers Change Lives

Giving can be broken down into several categories: time, talent, treasure, and gifts. Most of us are not great singers or speakers, but we all have time, some type of talent, some treasure, and spiritual gifts. When we choose to give these things away, we become powerful tools in the hand of God. This requires us to be unselfish givers, but that is what God is:

"For God so loved the world that he gave his one and only Son, that whoever believes in him shall not perish but have eternal life." (John 3:16)

God the Father is such a giver that He did not even hold back His own Son, but sent Him to die on the Cross so that we would have the opportunity to be forgiven. It is amazing that God the Father did this when He knew that millions of people would reject the sacrifice of Jesus. This should teach us that we should give also, even if others may reject what we give. Our giving should not be based on whether or not people will receive what we give; it should be based on giving people the opportunity to receive.

This may seem risky—and it is—but we will never know who will receive unless we give people an opportunity to reject our message, our love, our help, and us. Jesus gave without strings and without guarantees. Even though it's risky, the reality is that the more we give of ourselves, the more lives we will change. Let's get ready to give.

Chapter 14

Be a Hilarious Giver!

Remember this: Whoever sows sparingly will also reap sparingly, and whoever sows generously will also reap generously. Each man should give what he has decided in his heart to give, not reluctantly or under compulsion, for God loves a cheerful giver. And God is able to make all grace abound to you, so that in all things at all times, having all that you need, you will abound in every good work. (2 Corinthians 9:6-8)

Something Deeper Than Just Giving Away

We must have a proper view of giving. Godly giving often means sowing. When you just give something, it's gone and you don't expect anything from it, except perhaps to fill a need or bless someone. Sowing is a totally different process. Sowing means you give something in a way that you expect what you have given to grow or keep on benefiting in some way. We have all heard the old Chinese proverb: "Give a man a fish and you feed him for a day. Teach a man to fish and you feed him for a lifetime." The difference is either giving a temporary benefit or sowing a skill that continues to provide.

Will You Sow a Little or a Lot?

If someone plants (sows) one apple seed in the ground, the result is one apple tree. It will take that one seed about ten years before the tree itself begins to produce more seed. At the same time, someone else plants ten thousand apple seeds and has an apple orchard as far as the eye can see. They both had the same seeds. One person, however, sowed sparingly.

What will you do with what God has given you? Some of us don't have much money or even recognizable talent, but if you know Jesus, you have the one thing that literally billions of people don't have. If you know how to connect with Jesus, you have something more valuable than large financial holdings or abilities that impress people. But you have to sow. You may be a nobody in the world, but God takes nobodies and uses them to change the world every day, one life at a time. Don't worry about what you can't do; do what you can do!

Giving Is a Heart Issue

Anyone can be a giver. Anyone can give time, energy, and their God-given gifts to others. It is a choice and each of us must settle it in our own hearts.

> *Each man should give what he has decided in his heart to give, not reluctantly or under compulsion.* (2 Corinthians 9:7)

130

God doesn't twist people's arms to make them give. Whether it is our time, our talents, or our treasure, God has given them to us so we could change the world. He is very clear in His Word that we should tithe and give offerings, but He leaves the choice up to us. God is very concerned about our motives and attitudes. He wants us to cultivate the heart and attitude of a giver, or even better yet, a sower. As we live the life of a sower, we become like God in our attitudes and actions. As we sow into people, our churches, and our society, we should expect our efforts to bring forth change that will continue to reach more people and grow beyond our limited influence.

God also doesn't force us to have a *giver* attitude. It should not require people pushing and yelling at us to make us give. Too often this has been the case and it has made people reluctant to give their time, talents, and finances. Unfortunately, this hurts the person who is not giving as well as the person whom God had intended to receive.

Cheerful Giver

There is something wrong with a grumpy giver. Giving should bring joy and have no strings attached. The word *cheerful* in this passage can also be translated as *hilarious*. Just picture what the world would be like if everyone was giving with a hilarious attitude. What would happen if, instead of churches being filled with people trying to hold on to the little they had, they turned their eyes to a hurting world and gave with joy? What would happen is communities would begin to be changed, the power of God would move at all levels of society, and our churches would not be able to contain the people who were being blessed. If these people who had received then got a giving mind-set, this culture would continue to grow and the Church would be returned to a place of prominence and change in our society.

Remember That Sowing Is Better Than Just Giving

If you had a thousand dollars and handed it to a hungry, strung-out crack addict, that would be foolish. You could take that same money and sponsor a missionary for an entire year. Or you could support a youth ministry's outreach and see teenagers, who never heard a clear presentation of the gospel, give their lives to Christ. The difference shown in these examples is between giving as wasting, and giving as sowing. Obviously, the sowing has lasting benefits. God tells us to sow in good soil so He can produce a harvest in the days ahead.

Chapter 15

Don't Hold Back

People are passionate about many things such as relationships, careers, hobbies, making money ... and the list goes on. Deep within us is a need to be passionate—passionate in both giving and receiving. Passion drives people to go above and beyond what is normal. It can consume a person as they strive to live life to the fullest.

You Can See Passion

One of the most interesting things about passion is that you can see it. When someone is consumed with passion, it is very plain to see. The question is, "What makes people passionate?" Some people are naturally passionate. God has created them with a great degree of emotion and drive. Others become passionate after a particular experience. I know people who thought they were financially poor. After going to Third World countries, they realized what true poverty was. This left them with a changed perspective about their own situation, and, more importantly, a passion to help those in poverty.

Passion Received Must Be Passion Given Away

My life was radically changed when I received salvation through Jesus Christ. For the first time in my life I felt forgiven, cleansed, and most importantly, I felt peace. This was brought about by experiencing the love of God in my life. I began to understand the depth of God's love and passion toward me. At first this seemed strange. How could God love me and actually have passion toward me? But He had already demonstrated this to me when He sent His only Son to the Cross to pay for my sins. If God did not hold back even His own Son, He has passion toward you and me.

I also began to realize God had been drawing me closer and closer to himself through life's situations and circumstances. It amazed me that He was working behind the scenes while I was doing what I wanted to do without regard for Him or anyone else. As this continued to sink in, my love and adoration toward God grew. I became passionate about getting to know Jesus more and more. As I grew closer to Him and learned more about the depth of love He had for me, I began to become consumed with sharing Him with others.

We see it played out all the time in our lives. When you experience something great, you tell people about it. The latest CD, movie, or restaurant becomes the center of conversation. Last night's sitcom or music award show is passionately discussed. We want to share the joy and the experience of what we felt. We will share the things that made us feel good temporarily with so much enthusiasm.

How much more should we tell people about the greatness of God? How much more should we talk and brag about the eternal benefits of Jesus Christ? It honors God when we boldly declare His love and His plan for people. When God sees us glorifying Him, He steps beside us and co-labors with us as we share the good news.

The Greatest Commandment

Jesus amazed me with His response when the teacher of the Law asked Him what the greatest commandment was. He didn't give a list of what not to do; He gave a positive command of what we should do. He said, *"Love the Lord your God with all your heart and with all your soul and with all your mind and with all your strength"* (Mark 12:30). This is not a shy kind of love. It is not timid. It is bold, public, and unashamed. Jesus tells us to love God with all of our heart, emotions, intellect, and physical strength. We cannot and should not be outdone by people who are passionate about temporal or even sinful things.

Competing Messages

It is said that he who shouts loudest is heard. We live in a world that is shouting so many different messages. Between TV, radio, and everyone's opinions, we are bombarded night and day with diverse points of view. For many, it can be very difficult to weed through all of these attitudes. So when it comes to sharing the message of God's love, we have competition. Without passion and consistency, we will not succeed in sharing God's message with the world. But with passion and consistency, we can continuously lead people to Christ. In addition to the greatest commandment, Jesus gave us the Great Commission—to bring His message to the entire world.

Not the Great Suggestion

The Great Commission is not a suggestion. Jesus didn't say, "It would be nice if, in your spare time, you might put in a good word for Me if you feel like it." No, He told us to *go into all the world* and *make disciples*. This is where obedience comes in. In John 14:15 Jesus says, *"If you love me, you will obey what I command."* This makes it very clear that if we love Jesus, we must do our part in fulfilling the Great Commission in our lives.

Let the Soul Winners Dominate

For centuries, passive Christians have dominated Christianity. To begin with, "passive Christian" is an oxymoron. A true Christ-follower does the things that Jesus did. (See John 14:12.) Jesus was constantly winning people to His Father. He spent His time demonstrating the Kingdom of God in everyday culture and in people's lives. These new believers made the decision to spend their lives following Him instead of following any other philosophy or person. Jesus was a soul winner, just as we should be.

In the early Church, after the Day of Pentecost, the followers of Jesus were winning people to Him on a daily basis. This changed later when Christianity became the state religion of the Roman Empire and large cathedrals were built. People began to become passive in their faith, and it became normal for them to depend on their minister to do the work, instead of every believer being a minister.

The Power of Personal Evangelism

If everyone did his or her part, we could easily see the Great Commission completed in our lifetime. This is a demonstration of how it could be done within a few years if people made a decision to share their faith and win people to Jesus. Let me repeat the example I used in a previous chapter: Right now there are about six billion people on Earth. Of this number, there are currently over one billion born-again believers. If every follower of Christ got serious and made a decision to spend the next year winning just one person to Christ and teaching that person to share their faith, in one year one billion would become two billion believers. If these people made the same decision, in the second year, two billion would go to four billion. If this pattern continued, in the third year, that four billion could grow to include every single person on the face of the planet. This would be accomplished in only three years! Evangelism was not meant to be done by a few people with microphones, but by individuals who have the experience of salvation and have become determined to share God's plan with others.

Faith Is Best Shared With Those We Care About

Every day we are surrounded by people who are searching for meaning in their lives. They are in our families, at our jobs, and in our neighborhoods and towns.

They are available and, if we don't hide our faith, Christ is available to them when we share Him. The world is full of people who complain about our society and the trouble it faces. Millions of dollars are spent on man-made solutions when the issue is actually the heart—and only God can change the heart. God does the changing, but we are the spokesmen. We hear complaints about people, especially young people. If every adult would bring a child or a teen to church or win them to Christ in their neighborhoods, our nation would be radically changed as these children and teens would be launched into their God-given purposes. They would then become missionaries to their own generation. Some would say, "I don't want to be in youth ministry." You don't have to sign up to be in a ministry; you just have to share the love of Christ with one person.

Reason With People's Hearts and Souls

Too often we spend time reasoning with people's minds. The only problem is, God never told us to win people's minds, but to win their souls (see Proverbs 11:30). He also never told us to win arguments. We must boldly and unashamedly share the love of God without getting caught up in useless arguments. This does not mean that we don't share facts and truth in the form of apologetics, but before the conversation ends, the appeal must shift from the mind to the heart and soul. It has been said that people are eighteen inches away from Heaven. That's the eighteen inches between the head and the heart. Jesus may be in the mind, but not in the heart.

*That if you confess with your mouth, "Jesus is Lord,"
and believe in your heart that God raised him from
the dead, you will be saved.* (Romans 10:9)

As we share from our own hearts what God has done,
we will touch other people's hearts. People must believe
in their hearts, not just in their minds, and it often takes
a heart-to-heart exchange to really connect with people
emotionally and spiritually. It is easier to do with people
who have gained the trust that takes place in ongoing
relationships.

Infusing the Power, Plans, and Purpose of Jesus Into Our Culture

Infusion: "The process of injecting a substance to
increase effectiveness or bring change."

Our world desperately needs an infusion of Jesus
Christ. The only real way to change the world is to change
people's hearts. This change comes from the inside out, not
from a source working from the outside in. Individuals,
cultures, schools, businesses, and governments need the
power, purpose, and plans of Jesus Christ.

Too many individuals are living outside the purposes of
God and without God's power. This makes it impossible
for them to live out the plans for which God created them.
These broken, imperfect people then make up the families
and institutions that comprise our society.

We continually hear the statistics on crime, drugs, and
sexually transmitted diseases—all of which are the result

of people living outside God's intent. These problems are a result of the sin sickness from which we all suffer and need the cure of Jesus Christ to overcome. Disobedience to God, lack of understanding of Him, and the need for His direction is everywhere. Over time our families, institutions, and government have gotten further away from God, and our society reflects this. More police or government programs cannot solve the problem. The problem is the condition of people's hearts.

Our churches are meant to be spiritual hospitals, rehab centers, and training centers. Our churches should be producing individuals who carry and bring the purpose, power, and plans of Jesus Christ wherever they go. These individuals then become agents of change every day in our families, schools, businesses, and government.

Our churches have been holy huddles designed to help people escape the negative realities of society. This is not the purpose of the Church. In God's plan, the churches were never meant to be places of escape but, places of engagement. Individuals hear the message of Christ and choose to follow Him. They do this in a community or a church. Here they are trained to fix the problems of society, not to escape them. Jesus wasn't afraid of catching something; He was too busy trying to spread something!

It Takes More Than a Critic to Change the World

Our world is full of critics but has very few world-changers. Yes, we need to evaluate things, but more importantly we need to bring change to what we criticize.

It is very easy to sit around and point out the problems with people and our culture. It is very different to bring change. God has not called you to be a complainer, but to be a changer. The reason you are angry and frustrated by the way things are is because God wants you to be a part of the solution. God will allow you to walk in frustration until you get fired up enough to do something about it. The reason things have gotten so bad in certain areas of society is because there have been too many complainers and too few who understand the power of God and how it can change the world.

Overcoming the Feeling of Powerlessness

Others have tried to bring change and have not been able to. We have all tried in our own strength to change something and failed. We need to do two things to see real change: First, we have to rely on the power of God instead of on our own strength.

> *I can do all things through Christ which strengtheneth me.* (Philippians 4:13, KJV)

This helps us tremendously because it is not our own strength but God's that brings real change. Second, we need to join others and work together to advance God's Kingdom.

Either Be a World-Changer or Support and Partner With One

You may be reading this and know you are not the type of person who can lead a major movement to change the world. The reality is this is true for most people. But you do have a choice. You may not be called to lead a great move of God, but you can get behind someone who is called to lead in a major way. This doesn't make one person better than another; both people would just be walking out an assignment God gave them. In any great movement there are countless steps along the road to victory. Every step taken brings the task closer to its goal. Every step left undone stalls, or even stops, that goal from being accomplished.

If you are that rare person who is called to lead a major move of God, you will need many others to help you along the way. Building the right team, relationships, and support structure are all needed to do great things. We also need to be continually led by the Holy Spirit and God's Word along the way.

God's Direction Comes With God's Strength

Too often, people don't try to right wrongs or bring change because of the magnitude of the issue they face. The key is asking God where to focus and then proceeding in His guidance and strength. It's more about everyone doing their part than a couple of individuals doing mighty deeds.

Don't Go It Alone

While we learn to walk in God's strength and guidance more fully, God will also connect us with others. There is power in community. Our strength, resources, and the increased power of God can become powerful forces when we work together and continue to strengthen others as they join our cause. There also may be people doing right now what we have a passion for. If you have a passion to feed children in Africa, get involved with someone already ministering there. Go on a trip; see where you fit in. Maybe you are called to assist someone else. Maybe you will go, serve, and learn so that you can start your own organization. You might have a gift that someone else needs that will multiply their effectiveness. If you don't go, you will never know.

Reaching Youth

I minister to all ages, but the main purpose of my life has been to help teens succeed on all levels. Education, training, and advising are all important, but the most important is connecting them with Jesus Christ and helping them learn to follow Him. He has the strength and direction that we all need.

Going After the Youth Generation

To repeat my earlier statement, 90 percent of those who come to Christ do so before the age of twenty. What amazes me is that with a statistic like this, so many churches and individuals dedicate so little time and so few resources to reaching this group. After serving in full-time ministry for over ten years and working with so many churches, I have witnessed firsthand the lack of support for the ministries serving our youth. This is one of the main reasons many youth pastors and leaders do not serve more than a year or two. Youth ministry is one of the most stressful and least-supported ministries. This is unwise. Many churches are literally shrinking due to the death of older congregants and the fact that the church has not focused on winning the youth for decades.

While Hollywood, MTV, and the music industry daily spend millions to reach our youth and shape the way they think and live, many churches have no youth budget or ongoing productive ministry. This should not be.

The Birth of Fourth Generation Ministries

Instead of quitting or being frustrated with the reality that the culture is going after our teens with greater effectiveness than our churches, I began to formulate what eventually became Fourth Generation Ministries. I made a commitment to build youth ministries and churches that would cause them to pursue this generation with more passion than the secular world does. For this to happen, many connections and a great deal of resources would be needed. Fourth Generation was created as a nonprofit ministry with four focal points:

Teaching and Preaching God's Word—Through workshops, conferences, church services, and outreaches, God's Word goes forth, resulting in souls saved and disciples being made. One of the main goals is helping transition people from being spectator Christians into active soul-winners.

Leadership Training—When church and community leaders are strengthened, believers are equipped to bring change to individuals and communities.

Youth Ministry—Many youth outreaches and youth leadership trainings do not happen simply because of a lack of leadership or resources. This is unacceptable and Fourth Generation is committed to training leaders and bringing the gospel to all teens.

Urban Ministry—The greatest number of people and the major issues facing society are concentrated in our urban areas. In the early Church, the apostles went to the cities. If we want to affect society, we must focus on urban areas and especially on urban youth.

Fourth Generation Ministries exists to infuse our culture with the power, purpose, and plans of Jesus Christ. Fourth Generation was created to be a resource to the Body of Christ and society as a whole and is based on 2 Timothy 2:2: *"And the things you have heard me say in the presence of many witnesses entrust to reliable men who will also be qualified to teach others."*

The goals of Fourth Generation include winning souls to Jesus but, more importantly, to train people to be soul-winners and the hands and feet of Jesus in everyday life. We are not just called to teach God's Word, but to do it in such a way that results in creating other teachers who will continue to pass on the truth and power of God's Word to generation after generation.

Everyone Can Get Behind Youth Ministry

One of the tag lines I use at my local church is: "Whether face-to-face or behind the scenes, our teens need you." There are national trends that need to be confronted and it is going to take a massive effort on behalf of both people and our churches. I encourage all to do what they can to reach the youth in their communities or to support those who are committed to sharing Christ with teens and young adults.

Chapter 16

Do Something Great for God!

Such were the exploits of the three mighty men. Abishai the brother of Joab was chief of the Three. He raised his spear against three hundred men, whom he killed, and so he became as famous as the Three. He was doubly honored above the Three and became their commander, even though he was not included among them.

Benaiah son of Jehoiada was a valiant fighter from Kabzeel, who performed great exploits. He struck down two of Moab's best men. He also went down into a pit on a snowy day and killed a lion. And he struck down an Egyptian who was seven and a half feet tall. Although the Egyptian had a spear like a weaver's rod in his hand, Benaiah went against him with a club. He snatched the spear from the Egyptian's hand and killed him with his own spear. Such were the exploits of Benaiah son of Jehoiada; he too was as famous as the three mighty men. (1 Chronicles 11:19-24)

God has called His followers to do mighty deeds! What is God calling you to do? I have spent days as a follower of Christ endeavoring to help others or to lead a mighty move of God. God has a great exploit planned out for you. Ask Him to show you and He will.

Mission 10:20: Training 10,000 Leaders to Win 1,000,000 Souls by 2020

In the past several years God has opened up many doors of ministry for me. He has done amazing things in me and through me, many of which I did not expect or ask for, and most didn't even come about in the way I thought they would. In the fall of 2009, I hit a wall when I experienced a couple of disappointments while simultaneously having to make some major decisions about the direction of my life. I needed to know where God wanted me to focus. I was at a point where I had more opportunities than time or energy. Another reality was that every good thing that comes our way is not necessarily what God wants us to concentrate on. On top of that, I felt that God was directing me to make some decisions that didn't make sense to me. I pulled back to seek God and ask for His direction. What I got was a dream that has changed my life.

From a Troubling Dream to a Grand Vision

In my dream, I was driving down a road, past and through shadowy figures. As I was driving, I attempted

148

to hit the brakes but as I pressed with my foot, the brake pedal wasn't there. I then attempted to press the brakes with both feet and I still didn't stop. As I continued, my body slid entirely under the dashboard, but there were still no brakes and I couldn't stop. Then I woke up.

I don't often have dreams that I can remember when I wake up, and this dream shook me. As I sought the meaning through prayer and speaking with my senior pastor, the explanation of the dream became clear. In the dream, I was driving too fast and was going by and through people. I believed this meant God was telling me that while I was doing a great deal of ministry, I was not effectively reaching all the people that God had called me to impact. I was going too fast to be effective. God was telling me to slow down. More is not always better, especially in ministry. It is more important to be effective with a few than ineffective with many.

It also became clear that I am part of a movement that involves an army that is needed to reach the people represented in my dream. God desires to have an army of leaders and priests in order to reach a multitude that no man can number. If each Christian did their part and reached a few, the world would change sooner rather than later.

I was in a very emotionally tough spot. Certain things needed to change; my pace was unsustainable and not wise. I had people who wanted answers and in reality, I needed some answers myself. I had a burning desire to do all that God had put me on Earth to do and I knew that God was directing me to have clarity, but for the first time in my Christian life I was waking up night after night with multiple scenarios running through my head. For the first time in a long time, I hit a pause button so I could be still and hear the voice of God in these matters. I am beyond convinced that God speaks and directs His children, so I continued to seek His will.

Grassroots, underground, and underbelly

Later, during a period of prayer and fasting, God spoke three terms to me: *grassroots*, *underground*, and *underbelly*. God was telling me to focus on building a grassroots movement to strengthen our local churches. I'm affiliated with some large ministries that work on major events. This is important and part of God's plan to bring the gospel to large numbers of people at once. But God was letting me know that while I will continue to be involved in these events, my personal assignment was to help build leaders of local churches and ministries in a greater way. It is local churches and the ministries within them that do the discipleship and ongoing work of the Great Commission. Much of this is focused specifically on youth pastors who minister to teens. One of my greatest passions is to end spectator Christianity. If we can teach a generation to be passionate obedient followers of Christ now, it will change Church culture in our nation for decades to come. This can be stirred up, but will never be achieved at a single event or conference.

Grassroots

A grassroots movement of God must also be self-led and self-sustained. The most effective mission models go into people groups, identify and train local leaders who begin churches and ministries that will exist with or without external input. Much of our Christianity is event-based instead of people-based. Events come and go, but people in our communities and churches remain.

Underground

Underground was the next word. It means unrecognized. God was telling me to focus on promoting His will within people in ways that would not be obvious to outsiders. Changed lives are more important than high-profile events and ministries. There is nothing wrong with godly high-profile ministries and events, but God was telling me that much of my personal assignment would be in doing the things that would not be publicly recognized, but underground instead.

Underbelly

The last word was *underbelly*. To me this meant that I was to go after those people whom the Church was not reaching and some who would even be looked down upon. These include youth and youth culture, the down and outers, the up and outers, and those whom the average church person doesn't know how to reach, or in some cases, doesn't want to reach. God is concerned about all kinds of people, and too many churches don't want people in their congregations who do not fit in. The reality is that some people with the greatest call of God on their lives are wild in the world. They were created to do wild things for Jesus but as yet, they haven't been apprehended by God. Let the apprehension begin!

The Birth of Mission 10:20

God is not a small God. He does not have a small vision. We have been commanded to go into all the world and reach every group of people. I have a passion to see this happen in my lifetime. It is God's will and we need to get at it. Mission 10:20 was about to be birthed.

As I began to think and pray, I thought, *What if I could train 10,000 leaders in the next decade? What if they each committed to winning ten souls per year?* When you do the math, 10,000 youth pastors, pastors, and ministry leaders committed to winning ten souls per year equals 1,000,000 souls by 2020! When you look at the power of multiplication, you can see how the Great Commission can be fulfilled in our lifetime. This effort will be primarily focused on, but not limited to, youth. What would the New York metro region look like if one million teens were won to Christ and were discipled to walk in His power?

Okay, so I am a dreamer. Let's dream. Let's believe and bring the gospel to every human being. It will take all of us and we must each do our part, but it's not rocket science. It begins with each one of us seeking God every day, and God answering us and giving us more of His presence, power, and direction. We grow in that and share what we have with others who will also go and connect with Him in a greater way. It's about living for Christ every day.

Receive. Grow. Give it away....

Infusing the Purpose, Power, and Plans of Jesus Into Our Culture

We can do this right now. Today and every day, right where we are. We don't need a title or more direction; we have been commissioned. Don't be a spectator Christian! If God has been using you to reach people, pray that God uses you more. More importantly, help someone else grow to be a soul-winner and one who disciples others. Remember the Scripture that Fourth Generation Ministries is based on:

And the things you have heard me say in the presence of many witnesses entrust to reliable men who will also be qualified to teach others. (2 Timothy 2:2)

Paul was the first generation who taught Timothy. Timothy was the second generation, who was instructed to entrust reliable men with what he had received. These reliable men, who were the third generation, were then to teach the others, who became the fourth generation. This is a picture of what the culture of Christianity should look like. Generation after generation of believers who spend their lives building up a larger and stronger generation to follow.

If you are in ministry, you may not know where to start or how to get to the purposes of God that burn inside

153

you. Start with what you have, pour it into others, build up a team, and trust God for the increase.

Peer Mentoring and Learning Community

As I write this, I began this very morning a twelve-month Peer Mentoring and Learning Community with fifteen youth pastors and leaders from New Jersey. It was amazing to see how hungry these men of God were for legitimate relationships. These men are all gifted and called by God, but many are weary from continually pouring out without others pouring into them. We need to help each other along the road of life as we reach others for Christ. By deliberately pouring into these men for the next year, I am believing that they will become stronger men of God who will do great exploits in the days ahead. To the world, these men may be insignificant, but in God's view, they are called to reach literally hundreds or thousands of teens. By building relationships and community, God's power will move more powerfully.

Who is it that you can pour yourself into? Who can you connect with in your church, at your job, or in your community to do more together than you could ever do alone? Even though you have needs, you have gifts and qualities that others need. Share what you have, build others up, and trust God that both He and other believers will build you up where you need it.

Mission 10:20 Trainings in Newark, New Jersey—From Dream to Reality

When God gives you a vision, you have to act on it. As Mission 10:20 unfolded, I knew the first place I wanted to hold a training was in Newark, New Jersey. This is the largest city in New Jersey and one in which, historically, it has been difficult to reach the youth. I am believing that we can bring the gospel to every teen in Newark in a way they can understand. This will take hundreds of youth leaders to accomplish, but we are going to go for it. I am also committed to train leaders where others may not. Let's bring the gospel to every nook and cranny in our country. Whether it's a cornfield or the concrete jungle, let's bring it. I'm sharing my journey to encourage you. So I ask this question: "What is God directing you to do?" I have spent over a decade saying yes to God and doing things others said couldn't be done. What has God put on your heart to do? Be bold; do your part. God is waiting for you.

Working Together While Also Building Our Own Churches

Our goal is to strengthen the local youth and church leaders who are the ones ministering directly within the community. While each leader grows in their ability to evangelize their community and disciple their congregations, the effects will be cumulative. God has also been moving to unite the many churches of our region to work together in a greater way. This is happening in New Jersey and the five boroughs of New York. As the song says about New York, "If you can make it there, you can make it anywhere!"

What Are You Willing to Fight For?

The following is a story about one of David's mighty men who decided to stand his ground and fight for the territory on which he stood.

> *Next to him was Shammah son of Agee the Hararite. When the Philistines banded together at a place where there was a field full of lentils, Israel's troops fled from them. But Shammah took his stand in the middle of the field. He defended it and struck the Philistines down, and the LORD brought about a great victory.* (2 Samuel 23:11-12)

Shammah was willing to fight over a field of lentils? To the world, this field probably didn't matter, but it was Shammah's territory and the Philistines wanted to take it. God has given you a territory, and it is up to you to fight for it. Your territory represents the souls God has given you to reach or to strengthen. You may be like Shammah and everyone else may flee from the fight, but God will work a great victory through you.

Join Us!

If you are a ministry leader or an individual who wants to commit to winning ten souls a year, be a part of Mission 10:20 as it begins to unfold in 2010. God will use you greatly and together we can change our region for Jesus

Christ. There are two main ways you can be part of a big vision: First, you can either be a driving force behind the vision, or second, you can support someone and work with a vision-carrier. In God's eyes, position doesn't matter, just the outcome of changed lives.

If God called you to be the vision-carrier, lead others and help them grow as you work together to live out the vision. If you are not called to be the main vision-carrier, support someone who is. If you have that someone in your life, go for it and bring the vision to pass. If you want to be part of Mission 10:20, consider yourself invited. Get connected with us and trust God for the souls.

Many times after I preach, someone will come and tell me they liked my sermon. I then challenge them to follow through—just go do it! Some are excited; others are taken aback that I would put such a demand on them. Remember, God didn't call us just to hear His Word, but to do it.

So whatever you have received through reading this book, take the time to grow in the knowledge, understanding, and power of it. But more importantly, don't keep it to yourself. There is somebody waiting to receive what you have.

Every day when you wake up, take the things that God has given you, find someone who is spiritually hungry or thirsty, and give those things away.

Receive. Grow. Give it away ... until the world has heard the good news of Jesus Christ!

Appendix

Become an Infusion Partner

As I began to plan citywide youth events and leadership trainings, it became clear it would take much prayer and a lot of financial resources. You have the ability to support youth ministry through your prayers and financial support. By establishing Fourth Generation as a nonprofit organization, we created an avenue for people to sponsor youth events and leadership trainings that would not be possible without this type of support.

Support Every Season and Bear Fruit Every Season

One of our goals is to provide a realistic support plan for all people. Some people are able to give large, one-time donations; others can give on a monthly basis. Some have a heart to give, but monthly giving may not be possible. I know the reality of committing to a monthly pledge and then struggling or being unable to keep up to a personal commitment that has been made.

Infusion Partners

To make ongoing giving realistic for most people, we developed the Infusion Partnership. Infusion partners give $25 every three months, which is $100 a year. I believe God gave me this strategy as a means to have the constant income needed to plan, organize, and hold major youth events. Our goal is to be able to bring the gospel to all teens in both urban and non-urban areas without being restricted due to lack of finances.

I began to pray for one thousand people to commit to giving $100 a year. That would add up to $100,000 infused into youth ministry locally in the New Jersey and New York metropolitan region. I have never seen these types of resources committed to ongoing programs touching local communities and churches. This practical and achievable goal could change the face of youth culture in one of the most important regions in the world.

I have been accused of asking for too little from people, so right here and now I give you permission to give as much as you want. ("LOL," as the teens say.) All finances are directed to the four main purposes of Fourth Generation listed earlier. When you give, you are enabling more frequent, higher quality, and larger trainings and outreaches to take place. God wants to reach every teen with the power, purpose, and plans of Jesus Christ and to infuse these into our culture. Our team at Fourth Generation is committed to these goals, and we ask you to support us with your prayers and financial support. Please go to www.4thgen.org to learn more. Let's fulfill the Great Commission in our lifetime!

Other Books by Jack Redmond

People Matter to God

Experiencing Personal Transformation and
Sharing It With Others

Wounded Heart

Keys to Overcoming Life's Pain and Disappointments

These and other spiritual growth and discipleship
resources, such as training manuals and leadership
development tools, can be obtained at: www.4thgen.org.